Looking Back

A Photo Retrospective of the Mohawk Valley ~ Volume II

THE
OBSERVER-DISPATCH
uticaOD.com

FOREWORD

Each new day dawns with the opportunity for the Observer-Dispatch to tell the story of the people and places of this wonderful Mohawk Valley. Over a lifetime, or two, or three, those stories comprise a history of this place we treasure as our home.

Sometimes, those stories are best told in pictures – photos from family albums and old newspapers and yearbooks and private collections. It is our privilege and our pleasure to provide this historical, and pictorial, perspective of life in the Mohawk Valley.

We are appreciative of the assistance of the Oneida County Historical Society, and of the many readers who opened their files, their albums and their memories, to share these precious photos with others throughout the Mohawk Valley.

We hope you enjoy and reflect on the photos, as much as we did in compiling this book.

Donna M. Donovan
President and Publisher
The Observer-Dispatch/uticaod.com

INTRODUCTION

Why another pictorial history of the Mohawk Valley? There have been several in recent years – all well done and informative. "Looking Back: Mohawk Valley Vol. II," however, differs from others in a variety of ways.

It does not focus on any one community or particular section of the area and, instead, takes the reader on a journey through the entire region – from western Oneida County to Utica to Herkimer County, from Bridgewater and Waterville to the south to Remsen and Boonville to the north.

This book differs from others in another way, too. While it contains familiar photos of historic people, places and events that have appeared in the Observer-Dispatch and other books through the years, this book also contains dozens of photos submitted by residents of the region – photos that have been pasted in family al-

bums for years, just waiting for the chance to strut their stuff before many instead of few. This book gives them that opportunity.

There are photos of Mom and Pop posing in front of their grocery store or bakery or milk wagon or clothing store or tavern. There's the gang at the company picnic and a family enjoying the circus in town.

There's Johnny's Little League team, Aunt Sue's bowling team and the town's baseball team.

And there's Grandma and Grandpa with their eighth-grade graduating class. And Uncle Peter in front of his drums and other members of his high school band.

You, of course, get the picture … or pictures.

They come from the Oneida County Historical Society, the archives of the Observer-Dispatch and from you, the reader. It's a blend that results in an enjoyable journey down memory lane through the Mohawk Valley.

TABLE OF CONTENTS

Chapter One
VIEWS & STREET SCENES

If 10,000 years ago one were able to fly over what today is the Mohawk Valley, the scene would be very white. No green grass. No trees. No mountains. No valleys. No streams, rivers or lakes.

Just ice — ice many miles thick.

Then, the ice began to melt and retreat north and, in doing so, created the region we live in today.

Centuries ago, the region began to attract Native Americans from the Mississippi Valley. In the early 18th century came the first permanent settlers to the eastern section of the region and in the 1780s came settlers to the western section.

Since then and through the years, the region's landscape has changed dramatically.

Most area folks are familiar with pictures and postcards depicting those changes - the opening of the Erie Canal in 1825, the coming of the railroads in the 1830s, buildings big and small beginning to dot the area's cities, towns and villages and roads running through those communities.

Many photos in this chapter show those familiar scenes – and much more.

There is the old Erie meandering through the village of Ilion and there it is again, passing by the site where the Observer-Dispatch in Utica stands today. There's a plumber and butcher standing in front of their shops in Whitesboro.

We see Genesee Street in Utica in the early 20th century after a snow storm. And Utica's Busy Corner – at the intersection of Genesee, Lafayette and Bleecker streets – and learn how it got its nickname.

The region's roads, once narrow, bumpy, muddy and unpaved, were transformed when they began getting the first coat of macadam to accommodate the growing number of horseless carriages that were starting to appear.

ABOVE: Ilion in the late 1800s, including the Erie Canal. Ilion's relationship with the canal lasted exactly 100 years. Navigation through the village began in 1821 and continued until 1921 when the canal was abandoned. *Courtesy Mel and Evelyn Edwards*

RIGHT TOP: Erie Canal and John Street intersection in Utica in 1895. Today the buildings are the site of the Observer-Dispatch and its visitor's/employee parking lot facing John Street. *Courtesy Observer-Dispatch archives*

RIGHT BOTTOM: Lafayette Street in Utica, including the Hippodrome Theatre at left, circa 1900. *Courtesy Diana C. Howard*

BELOW: The Busy Corner in Utica, circa 1900. *Courtesy Mel and Evelyn Edwards*

ABOVE: Upper Genesee Street in Utica, circa 1905. *Courtesy Mel and Evelyn Edwards*

TOP LEFT: The Erie Canal near Utica, circa 1905. *Courtesy Diana C. Howard*

LEFT: Genesee Street in Utica after a heavy snow in the early 1900s. *Courtesy Oneida County Historical Society*

ABOVE: The Savings Bank of Utica on Genesee Street in Utica, circa 1910. Courtesy Mel and Evelyn Edwards

BELOW: Genesee Street looking south from the Erie Canal Bridge in Utica, circa 1910. Courtesy Mel and Evelyn Edwards

ABOVE: The Fulton Block, at Main and Moseley streets in Whitesboro, housed three businesses at the time this photo was taken in 1906. Frank O'Brien, a plumber, and John Brimson, a butcher, occupied the first floor. A printer occupied the second floor. Courtesy Whitesboro Historical Society

ABOVE: Columbia Street in Utica, circa 1910.
Courtesy Diana C. Howard

LEFT: Bleecker Street in Utica, circa 1910.
Courtesy Mel and Evelyn Edwards

BELOW: A panoramic view of Utica including a bird's eye look down Genesee Street, circa 1905.
Courtesy Mel and Evelyn Edwards

ABOVE: Clinton Street in New York Mills, looking north, circa 1910.

Courtesy Mel and Evelyn Edwards

RIGHT TOP: Main Street in Alder Creek, circa 1912.

Courtesy Oneida County Historical Society

RIGHT BOTTOM: The intersection of Genesee, Bleecker and Lafayette streets in downtown Utica has been called the Busy Corner for more than 100 years and this photo shows why. Trolley tracks from all directions converged on the corner, each day moving dozens of electric trolley cars filled with downtown workers, shoppers, theatergoers, diners and those with appointments with the many doctors, lawyers, accountants and other professional people with offices in the business district. This photo was taken on May 20, 1941, just eight days after the trolleys stopped running and were replaced by motor buses. On May 13, workers with Mid-State Builders, N. D. Peters Company and the Works Progress Administration (a federal agency that provided work for the unemployed on public works projects) began to remove trolley tracks and pavement bricks and construct a concrete pavement base for an asphalt top. Workers were kept busy all summer removing tracks and paving streets.

Courtesy Oneida County Historical Society

BELOW: Oneida Street from Jewett Place in Utica, circa 1915.

Courtesy Mel and Evelyn Edwards

ABOVE: Downtown Utica had many busy sections in the years after the end of World War II in 1945, but none busier than the block between Elizabeth and Bleecker streets — shown here looking north. The 14-story First National Bank Building, on the right, was the home of Kresge's five and dime on the ground floor. The building's upper-floor offices housed dozens of lawyers and companies. That's Charles Morrow's Nut House on the left where one could buy everything from peanuts and cashews to almonds and walnuts. The block also was the home of such places as Woolworth's, Liggett's drug store, Kittenger's department store, Doyle-Knower women's clothing, Fiemma Brothers shoes, Thom McAn's shoes and Daniels Jewelers. *Courtesy Observer-Dispatch archives*

LEFT: Varick Street has changed through the years, but it always has been one of the busiest sections of Utica. It is named for Abraham Varick Jr., who moved to Utica from Hackensack, N.J., in 1804 and quickly became a successful businessman. He was one of the first to buy and develop land in West Utica. His wife, Ann, was the daughter of William Floyd of Westernville, one of the four New Yorkers to sign the Declaration of Independence in 1776. This 1954 scene shows Varick Street south from Columbia Street. The southwest corner was occupied for years by Nick Pole's restaurant, the Varick Hotel, William Weir's drug store, the Rainbow Restaurant and Walter Sutkowski's dry goods store. *Courtesy Observer-Dispatch archives*

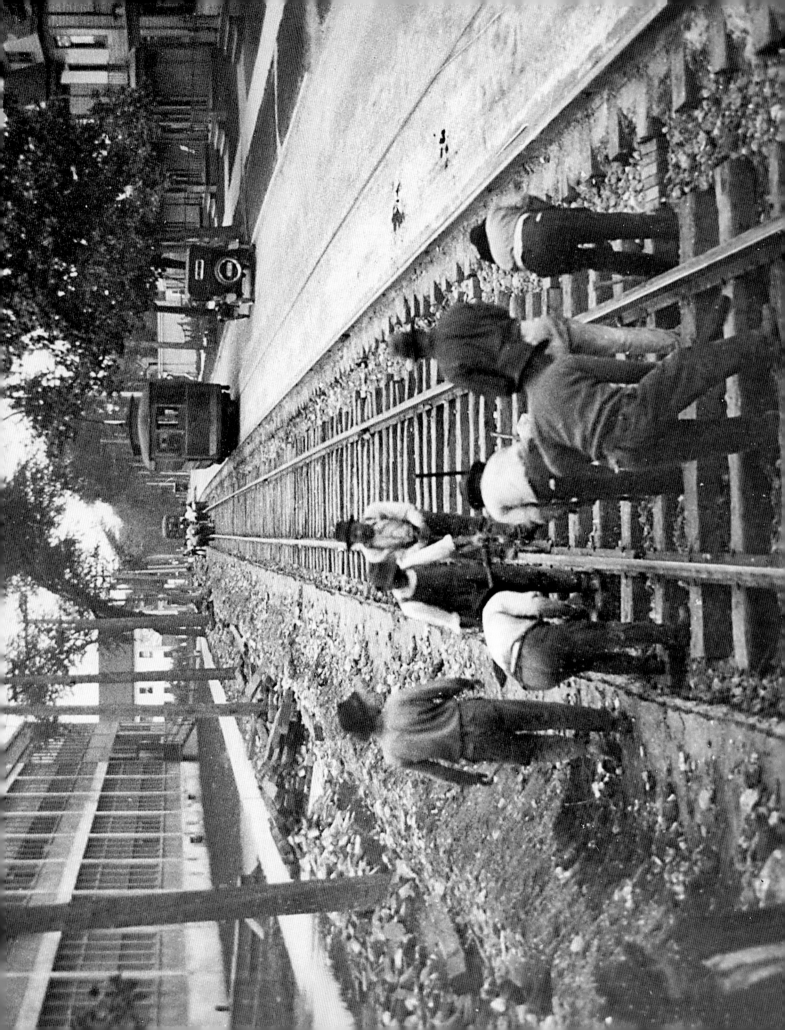

Chapter Two

TRANSPORTATION

Before the Mohawk Valley region became home to the Erie Canal in the 1820s, the Utica & Schenectady Railroad in the 1830s and modern highways in the 1900s, the village of Utica was a major transportation center.

In the late 18th and early 19th centuries, hundreds of westbound pioneers – many from New England heading to the territories of Michigan, Illinois and Indiana and beyond – would arrive in Utica via the Mohawk River or King's Highway from Albany. In Utica they would get on the Seneca Turnpike and travel south and then west to their destinations by wagon.

Many travelers would stay in Utica overnight or longer to prepare for the long, arduous journey ahead. To accommodate them, there sprung up hotels, inns, taverns, wagon repair shops, grocery store and dry goods stores in Utica.

Transportation had become a major industry in the region.

And the industry grew as the years passed by.

First came the Erie Canal in 1825, then the railroads in the 1830s and lateral canals in the 1840s (such as the Chenango Canal from Utica south to Binghamton and the Black River Canal from Rome north to Lyons Falls).

Later in the century came the trolleys, first horse-drawn and later powered by electricity.

The 20th century brought with it the automobile, the airplane, better roads and, in the 1950s, the Governor Thomas E. Dewey Thruway.

This chapter contains many pictures and postcards of residents of upper Mohawk country on the move.

Through the years, transportation has played an important role in the growth and prosperity of the region. It continues today to contribute to the economic well-being of the area.

OPPOSITE: For nearly 78 years—from Sept. 14, 1863 to May 12, 1941—trolleys in the Utica area carried thousands of passengers a day to work, to stores and to play. By 1920, the Utica Belt Line had 185 cars operating on 131 miles of track and employing about 900. This photo shows workmen repairing tracks along Bleecker Street — looking west — near Culver Avenue. The trolley era ended when along came the Great Depression, the motor bus and automobile. At midnight on Monday, May 12, 1941, the City Hall bell tolled farewell as Mayor Vincent R. Corrou — wearing a gold-plated operator's cap — joined Motorman Peter Ballsizer and piloted the last trolley car from the Busy Corner east along Bleecker, past the Masonic Home and into a car barn near Forest Park. The trolley era had reached the end of the line.

Courtesy Oneida County Historical Society

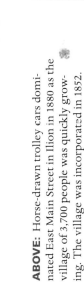

ABOVE: Horse-drawn trolley cars dominated East Main Street in Ilion in 1880 as the village of 3,700 people was quickly growing. The village was incorporated in 1852.
Courtesy Oneida County Historical Society

TOP RIGHT: Horse-drawn trolley cars operated in Utica from 1863 to 1890. On March 18, 1890, electric trolleys began to rule the road. One thing, however, did not change. Trolley tracks had to be cleaned frequently. In the 1870s and 1880s, that job was the responsibility of Driver William E. Curran and his 10-horse team that pulled a large sweeper. This photo shows the sweeper with the Marble Block - on the west side of Lower Genesee Street - in the background. It was not far from today's Commercial Travelers Mutual Insurance Company. Some of the businesses there in the 1880s included Walter North, photographer; George Wescott's caps, hats and furs; George Clark's variety store and the Roberts, Butler clothing shop.
Courtesy Oneida County Historical Society

RIGHT: Putnam's Creamery at 1417 Utica Street in Oriskany, circa 1885. The creamery was known for its ice cream. Courtesy Shirley Burtch

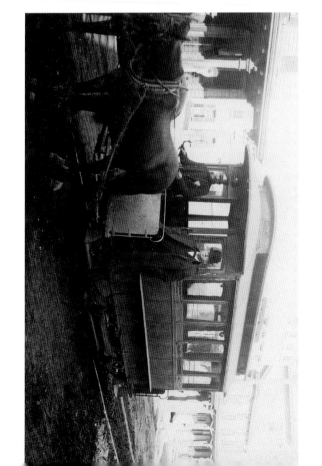

ABOVE: The lock at Frankfort on the Erie Canal, circa 1900 *Courtesy Mel and Evelyn Edwards*

LEFT: This unique bicycle built for 10 made several appearances in Utica in the late 1800s. It was designed by Charles Herman 'C.H.' Metz, who was born in Utica, October 17, 1863. *Courtesy Oneida County Historical Society*

BOTTOM LEFT: A trolley rounds the corner at Forest Park in Utica, circa 1905. *Courtesy Mel and Evelyn Edwards*

BELOW: Horse-drawn Deerfield streetcar, circa 1905. *Courtesy Mel and Evelyn Edwards*

RIGHT: State road-building crew at Augusta, September 30, 1907.

Courtesy Oneida County Historical Society

BELOW: The first official train over the electrified West Shore Railroad that ran between Utica and Syracuse, June 15, 1907.

Courtesy Mel and Evelyn Edwards

LEFT: Gaylord Jones in front of his delivery wagon, circa 1908. He carried mail and passengers between Rome and North Western.
Courtesy Mel and Evelyn Edwards

BOTTOM LEFT: Uticans got their first close-up look at an airplane when aviator Eugene Godet put on a flying demonstration in Roscoe Conkling Park, September 16, 1911. More than 25,000 people gathered to see Godet take off and land several times and fly over the area.
Courtesy Mel and Evelyn Edwards

BELOW: Unidentified men work on their early airplane in Summit Park in Oriskany, circa 1911.
Courtesy Mel and Evelyn Edwards

RIGHT: Motorcyclists line up on Elizabeth Street in Utica, circa 1912. Courtesy Oneida County Historical Society

BOTTOM RIGHT: Horses, automobiles, bicycles and trolleys share the road in Rome, 1915. Courtesy Oneida County Historical Society

BELOW: Train depot in Chadwicks, circa 1915. Courtesy Oneida County Historical Society

ABOVE: New York Central Railroad's Union Station in Utica, circa 1921. *Courtesy Mel and Evelyn Edwards*

BELOW: For more than 50 years, a familiar sight for residents of New York Mills was Trolley No. 12 rumbling along the bridge over Sauquoit Creek in the village at the intersection of Burrstone Road and Main and Clinton streets. The trolley would travel to Henderson Street and then to the vicinity of the Sadaquada Golf Club where it would turn around and head back to Utica. The building in the background of the photo is the textile mill in the upper section of the village. Trolley service - first with horse-drawn cars and later with electric cars - began in New York Mills on June 21, 1887 and ended on July 5, 1938. Record-breaking trolley traffic in the Utica area occurred in 1918 during World War I when nearly 29 million passengers rode the rails to work, to shop and to get to recreational spots such as Summit Park in Oriskany and Utica Park. By 1920, the Utica lines had 185 trolley cars, operating along 131 miles of track and employing 857 persons. Then, in the late 1920s, more and more motor vehicles began to hit the road. Trolleys began to be replaced by buses. On May 12, 1941, the area's last trolley rolled off into the sunset. *Courtesy Oneida County Historical Society*

ABOVE: The old Number 4 trolley heads south on Genesee Street, in Utica. Until service ended in the late 1930s and early 1940s, trolleys carried thousands of Mohawk Valley passengers to work, shopping area, parks and picnic grounds. *Courtesy Oneida County Historical Society*

TOP: Open trolley cars in days of old were fine in pleasant weather, but not so comfortable when it rained. As the late Robert G. Gurley wrote in his 1964 booklet "Here Comes the Trolley!" - an illustrated history of the electric trolleys in Utica - side curtains kept most of the passengers dry during rain storms, but not so the motorman. He got wet. On summer days when all seats were filled, passengers were permitted to stand on "running boards" along the side of the car. Electric trolleys first appeared in Utica in 1890. The last one ran May 12, 1941. *Courtesy Observer-Dispatch archives*

ABOVE: A Utica Transit Company bus picks up passengers in Downtown Utica in the 1950s. Courtesy Oneida County Historical Society

BELOW: A Cessna airplane at the old Utica Municipal Airport in Marcy, circa 1945. The plane went into a skid on takeoff and landed upside down. Bartnick's Garage in Utica sent a tow truck and got the plane back upright. No one was injured. Courtesy Shelly Bartnick

ABOVE: London Midland and Scottish Railway Royal Scot Class 6100 was an exhibition locomotive that toured North America in the early 1930s and is shown here at Utica's Union Station where it attracted large crowds. Courtesy Oneida County Historical Society

BELOW: Frank Ferro looking at a car stuck in the snow in Utica, early 1940s. Courtesy Sandra Ferro

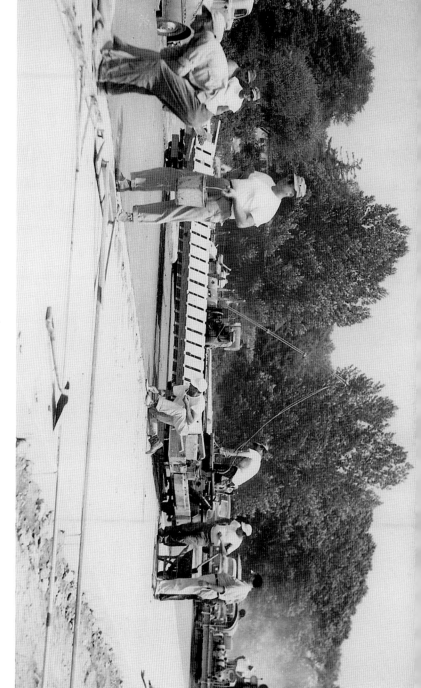

THIS PAGE: New York State Thruway construction in the 1950s. *Courtesy Oneida County Historical Society*

Chapter Three
SCHOOLS & EDUCATION

7he reader will not see many school buildings in this chapter, but will come face to face with faces — faces galore of hundreds of young people posing with classmates from schools across the Mohawk Valley region.

The collection of photos also includes some of the area's top-notch sports teams through the years.

Education in the region, especially higher education, has come a long way in its nearly 300-year history.

School classes in the early 1800s in what is now Herkimer County and in the early 1700s in what is now Oneida County were usually held in church halls, court rooms or in small log cabins.

The schools were private in those days since there were no public schools. And, they were "for boys only."

When parents began to complain and demand that their daughters get an education, too, female academies began to open. For years, the only colleges in the region were Hamilton College (chartered in 1793) and the Fairfield Medical College in Herkimer County (that no

longer exists). Both were all-male at the time.

The Oneida Institute of Science and Industry, off Main Street in Whitesboro, was founded in 1827 by Presbyterians in the area "to educate young men who have ultimately in view the gospel ministry." It was called a "school of higher learning" and most scholars today agree that it was the first such school in the United States to admit African-Americans on an equal footing with whites.

Today, two- and four-year colleges dot the area and not only provide a higher education for thousands but also pour millions of dollars a year into the local economy. They include Utica College, SUNYIT, Hamilton College, Mohawk Valley Community College, Herkimer County Community College, the Utica School of Commerce, the St. Elizabeth Medical Center's School of Nursing and Pratt at Munson-Williams-Proctor Institute. And, of course, there are the region's neighbors: Colgate University and SUNY at Morrisville.

ABOVE: Cecily Baker's Private School students with their teacher, circa 1890. The school was on Court Street in Utica.
Courtesy Laura Perkins

TOP RIGHT: South Street School students in Utica, circa 1892.
Courtesy Oneida County Historical Society

RIGHT: Utica Business College students, circa 1900.
Courtesy Oneida County Historical Society

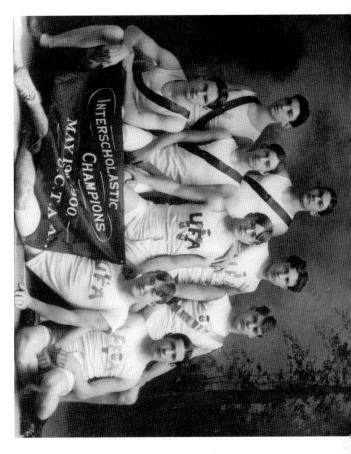

ABOVE: Deerfield Grad School graduation, 1905. Note each student is wearing a ribbon.
Courtesy Laura Perkins

TOP: The Utica Free Academy Interscholastic champion track team of 1900.
Courtesy Oneida County Historical Society

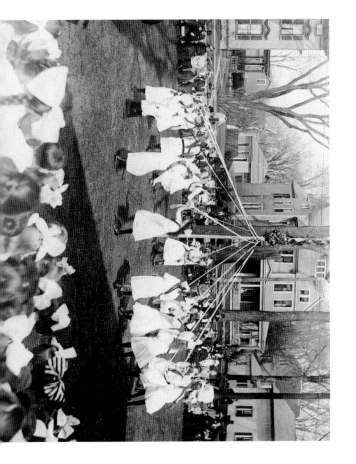

ABOVE: Hamilton College track team, circa 1901. Courtesy Oneida County Historical Society

BELOW: Maypole dance on front lawn of the school known as the 'Old Green School,' on Main Street in Whitesboro, May 5, 1916. Courtesy Whitesboro Historical Society

ABOVE: Holland Patent grades 1-3 in front of Village Hall, circa 1919. Among those pictured are Bill Hughes, Stephen Sobolowski and Doris Zimmerman.
Courtesy Oneida County Historical Society

TOP RIGHT: Oriskany High School basketball team of 1923. The Oriskany school did not have a gym so the team practiced in Cole's Ice House which was the only building in town large enough. Later they were permitted to use the basketball court in the Whitestown Town Hall. During the winter, the team would ice skate to their practices on the abandoned Erie Canal, carrying the basketball in a sack. Front row, from left: Philip Carpenter, Kenneth Allen, Thurlow Cook, Arnold O'Neil, John Cole. Back row, from left: Jack Patterson, Stanley Phillips, David Chamberlin, Principal Raymond Smith. *Courtesy Shirley Burtch*

RIGHT: The Utica Free Academy band in 1925. *Courtesy Observer-Dispatch archives*

ABOVE: Sacred Heart School graduation, Utica, 1930. *Courtesy Diane Lange*

LEFT TOP: The 100-bed Utica Memorial Hospital at 1634 Genesee St. is gone, but continues to be remembered fondly by many. It opened in 1895 followed by its school of nursing in 1899. In the late 1950s, it merged with St. Luke's Hospital in a new facility on Champlin Avenue known as the St. Luke's Memorial Hospital Center. Shown here are nursing graduates in the Class of 1930 and their supervisors. From left, standing: Dietitian Gladys Ertz, Etoila Marsh, Alice Smith, Ruth Mahaffy, Viola Rowlands, Supervisor Gladys E. Rice, Supervisor Grace Landon, Supervisor Alma Barnes, Supervisor Dorothy McBride, Geneva Eldred, Viola Hawley, Helen Evans, Supervisor Lorena Reilly and Supervisor Isabelle Miller Lewis; seated: Sophye Altshuler, Leona Harris, Estelle Dodge, Lucille Hanley, Supervisor Olivia Cuppen, Supervisor Julia Hardy, Marguerite Maier, Margaret Ames, Anna Hobica and Genevieve Frank. *Courtesy Utica Memorial Hospital Alumni Association*

ABOVE: Cast of "Melinka of Astrakhan," New Hartford High School, March 10, 1934. *Courtesy Oneida County Historical Society*

RIGHT: The first grade class of 1935-36 at Blessed Sacrament School on James Street in Utica. Bill Chanatry is in the third row from the left, fourth seat from the front. *Courtesy Bill Chanatry*

ABOVE: Students outside Remington Rand Sales Training School in 1942.
Courtesy Oneida County Historical Society

RIGHT TOP: Evelyn R. Edwards of Clinton, in her book, 'The Sauquoit Valley', says that Chadwicks High School graduated its last class in 1984 and eventually the Chadwicks Union Free School District became part of the Sauquoit Valley Central School District. The original Chadwicks school was built in 1914-15 and additions were built in 1930 and in 1973. Through the years, the school had some great sports teams. Cheering the varsity and junior varsity squads during the 1941-42 season were, from left, Margaret Shaul, Mary Alice Sweet (Gray), Joyce Richards (Shephard), Mary Bristol (Suplee), Bonnie Bedford (Nuccio), Tom Sweet. Lois Onyan (Kogut), Alene Hughes (Clough), Amelia Hanus, Helen Szancilo, Shirley Bauer (Slasko) and Frances Shaul (Kozak). *Courtesy Oneida County Historical Society*

RIGHT BOTTOM: The 8th grade graduating class at Wetmore School in East Utica in 1948. The school was built in 1900 and closed in the mid-1990s. *Courtesy Oneida County Historical Society*

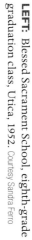

LEFT: Blessed Sacrament School, eighth-grade graduation class, Utica, 1952. *Courtesy Sandra Ferro*

BOTTOM LEFT: St. Agnes basketball team, Utica, 1951. Front row, left to right: Albert Mazloom, Paul Lange, Terry Murphy, Bill Chambrone and Tom Mahar. Back row, Cosmo Saraceno (coach), Bill Walsh, Eddie Masohn, Anthony Tresoline, Terry Green, Dan Salvo and Rev. Thomas Guyder. *Courtesy Diane Lange*

BELOW: Utica Free Academy basketball team in 1955. They were city champions. *Courtesy Wayne Decker*

WATCH THIS WINDOW
FOR FRIDAY AND SATURDAY SPECIALS
Carnation Milk
From Contented Cows
Pure- Double Rich!
3 FOR 31¢
FRESH
SHOULDER
19¢
Carnation
MILK
CARNATION
MILK

Chapter Four

COMMERCE

Frrom the very beginning in the 18th century, when permanent settlers first began to build their homes in upper Mohawk country, some of them had goods and services to sell to their neighbors. And their neighbors were eager to buy those goods and services.

Commercial enterprises in the region date back that far and as the area grew in population, so did the number of such enterprises.

Early in the region's history, the number of grocery stores, dry goods stores, blacksmith shops, wagon repair shops, hotels, taverns, inns and restaurants multiplied rapidly to not only serve the residents in the area, but also to accommodate the hundreds of westbound travelers who passed through the area and were eager to buy

goods before continuing their journey.

By the 19th and 20th centuries, the region was dominated by hundreds of mom and pop stores. They were the mainstays of the neighborhoods, where relatives and friends gathered every day to buy groceries, meats, baked goods, candy and produce – and exchange gossip. There were the corner taverns, barber shops, beauty salons where old friends met to enjoy a drink, get their hair cut — and exchange gossip.

This chapter contains many photos of those small stores and the moms, pops and their children who worked long hours to make them profitable.

There are, of course, photos of larger commercial enterprises – such as car dealers, banks, bowling alleys, furniture stores and newspapers.

OPPOSITE: Guarnieri's Market on the corner of Blandina and Bacon streets in Utica, circa 1924. This photo was submitted by Carmen Guarnieri, the son of the proprietor. Pictured, counterclockwise from right: Joseph Guarnieri, proprietor; Vito Guarnieri, partner; Joseph Romanelli; and Frank Romanelli. Joseph Guarnieri ran the shop through the Depression era until 1939. As a child, Carmen remembers sitting on 100-pound bags of sugar kept behind the counter. He would watch customers and draw to pass the day. Courtesy Carmen Guarnieri

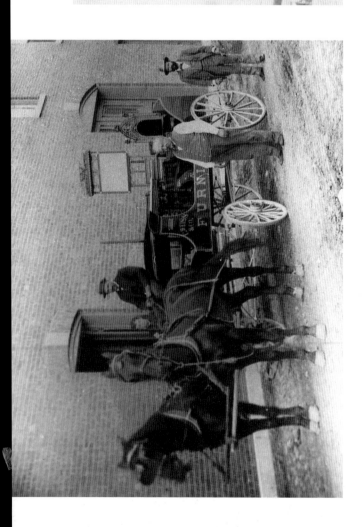

ABOVE: After closing his first store in Paris Station in 1890, a new store was built by Lincoln Davies. This store is in use today with additions having been built on to the original structure over the years.

Courtesy Max Townsend

BELOW: Field and Start wholesale groceries in Utica, circa 1896.

Courtesy Oneida County Historical Society

ABOVE: 1890 photo of Christian Weiss & Company furniture store's two-horsepower delivery wagon and employees in front of the entrance to the factory and salesroom at 11-13 State Street in Utica. Courtesy Oneida County Historical Society

RIGHT: Bakery on Oneida Square owned by George H. Harris, circa 1894. George is standing in the doorway. His wife Elizabeth is in the window and four of their six children are standing out front.

Courtesy Jan Harris Dudajek

34

ABOVE: Utica Trust and Deposit Company Bank, circa 1910. *Courtesy Mel and Evelyn Edwards*

RIGHT TOP: Coopers Store on Whitesboro Street in the Hall Block, Yorkville, Town of Whitestown, 1903. This was a general store that sold everything from groceries and soap to nuts. It was owned by Robert Cooper (Civil War veteran), and worked by his sons, Robert Rallo and William. The store was destroyed by fire and was moved a short distance to Main Street. *Courtesy Beverly R. Miller*

RIGHT BOTTOM: Bissell and Sons Stores in Waterville, circa 1900. The Bissell store opened in 1852 and remained in business until 1953, after 101 years of continuous operation. The brick building at left was a grocery and hardware store. The wooden two-story building at right was a drug store. *Courtesy Oneida County Historical Society*

35

ABOVE: Carr's Candy Store on Lafayette Street in Utica, circa 1912. The store was owned by Francis Carr and was located across the street from Hotel Utica. George Harrison Harris and his mother-in-law, Winifred Carr, are at the back of the store. *Courtesy Jan Harris Dudajek*

BELOW: Offices of Field and Start wholesale groceries at 42-50 John Street in Utica, October 1915. W. Henry Start is at left. Ervin C. Field is seated center. *Courtesy Oneida County Historical Society*

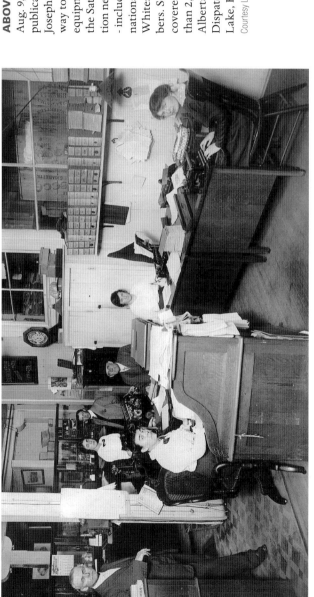

ABOVE: A sad item appeared in the Observer-Dispatch on Aug. 9, 1924: "The printing press and linotypes used in the publication of the Utica Saturday Globe have been sold to Joseph Fiske, of Newark, N.J., and their dismantling got under way today. Fiske is starting The Press, a tabloid, and Globe equipment will be moved there." From 1881 to the early 1920s, the Saturday Globe was sold across the country with circulation nearing 300,000. Its color illustrations attracted readers - including Queen Victoria - and it became the country's first national newspaper. Posing in front of its offices and plant on Whitesboro Street in 1915 were nine of its many staff members. Seated, from left, Hugh P. McCabe, famed reporter who covered the Johnstown (Pa.) flood in 1889 that claimed more than 2,000 lives; editor Albert M. Dickenson and reporter Alberta Dickenson, who later reported for the Observer-Dispatch. Standing from left, John Cogley, Harry Gowley, Fred Lake, Harry Johnston, John O'Hanlon and Walter H. Main. *Courtesy Laura Perkins*

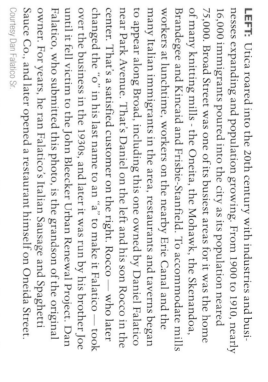

LEFT: Utica roared into the 20th century with industries and businesses expanding and population growing. From 1900 to 1910, nearly 16,000 immigrants poured into the city as its population neared 75,000. Broad Street was one of its busiest areas for it was the home of many knitting mills - the Oneita, the Mohawk, the Skenandoa, Brandegee and Kincaid and Frisbie-Stanfield. To accommodate mills workers at lunchtime, workers on the nearby Erie Canal and the many Italian immigrants in the area, restaurants and taverns began to appear along Broad, including this one owned by Daniel Falatico near Park Avenue. That's a satisfied customer on the right. Rocco — who later changed the "o" in his last name to an "a" to make it Falatico — took over the business in the 1930s, and later it was run by his brother Joe until it fell victim to the John Bleecker Urban Renewal Project. Dan Falatico, who submitted this photo, is the grandson of the original owner. For years, he ran Falatico's Italian Sausage and Spaghetti Sauce Co., and later opened a restaurant himself on Oneida Street.
Courtesy Dan Falatico Sr.

BOTTOM LEFT: Charlie Davis and his wife in the Wind's Bakery delivery wagon, Whitesboro, July 24, 1915. They are in front of the barn on Main and Clinton streets. *Courtesy Whitesboro Historical Society*

BELOW: The St. James Hotel in Utica, circa 1920. Built in 1886, this hotel stood for nearly 110 years on the north side of Whitesboro Street just west of Bagg's Square. *Courtesy Mel and Evelyn Edwards*

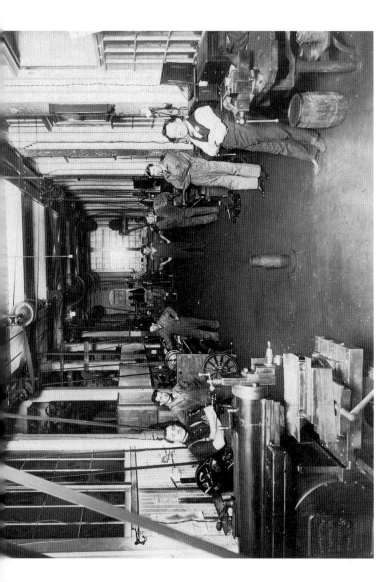

ABOVE: Lincoln Davies store in Paris Station began moving from horses to trucks in the early 1920s. To fuel the trucks, gas pumps were added. *Courtesy Max Townsend*

BELOW: Original location of Bick & Heintz, Inc. on Schuyler Street in Utica, 1925. On the left is Aldis Heintz and Henry A. Bick, right, founders of this business. *Courtesy Bick & Heintz, Inc*

ABOVE: Interior of Crank's Garage on Hotel Street in Utica, circa 1920. *Courtesy Oneida County Historical Society*

BELOW: Tow truck in front of Bick & Heintz, Inc. on Stark Street in Utica, 1942. From left: Bill Reinhardt, Henry Seeger, Bob Anacker and Robert J. Bick. Joe Schram is in the truck. The business is still located on Stark Street and Robert J. Bick continues to be active in the company. *Courtesy Bick & Heintz, Inc*

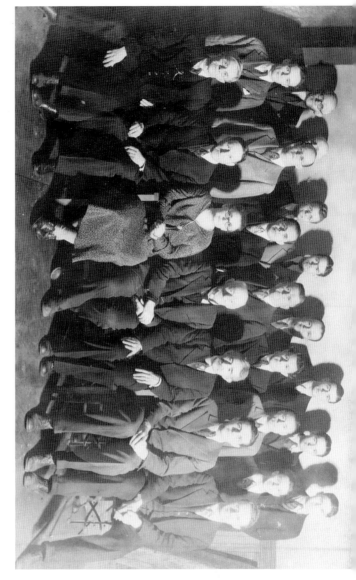

ABOVE: H. D. Morehouse and Sons appliance dealership on Columbia Street in downtown Utica, circa 1928. Included in the photo are Frank Carter, Chic Emerson, Marshall Longway, Les Morehouse, Jim Longway, and Dick Richards. *Courtesy Henry Moorehouse*

TOP LEFT: Employees of the Utica Daily Press in the mid-1920s. In the back row is Arthur J. 'Bud' Carl. Middle row, fourth from left is Pat Carney. *Courtesy Charles A. Carl*

LEFT: New truck delivered to Lincoln Davies store in Paris Station in 1926. *Courtesy Max Townsend*

RIGHT: Downtown Utica in 1928. In its heyday, Woolworth's five-and-dime had 2,100 variety stores throughout the world. And it all began in Utica in 1879 when Frank W. Woolworth opened his first store on Bleecker Street. Woolworth's had several locations in Utica through the years before opening a modern store in 1940 on the east side of Genesee Street between Bleecker and Elizabeth streets. In 1928, it was a couple of doors below - at 167 Genesee - and its neighbor one floor above was the Asia Restaurant and above it was Sam Furcinito's Palace Bowling Academy. Woolworth's closed its Utica stores in 1997 and most of its other stores at about the same time.

Courtesy Stanley and Craig Mielnicki

TOP RIGHT: Sperrys Agency Insurance, Real Estate, Notary and Town Clerk, Whitesboro, circa 1929. The business was on Main Street. Courtesy Whitesboro Historical Society

LEFT: Frank Ferro, left, in front of Oneida County Creameries Co., Utica, early 1930s. Courtesy Sandra Ferro

BELOW: Robert Coopers & Son Grocery Store on Main Street in Yorkville, Town of Whitestown, 1930. The store was on Whitesboro Street until it was destroyed by fire. Coopers was the only general store in Yorkville until it closed in 1948. Courtesy Beverly R. Miller

ABOVE: Offices of the Utica Observer-Dispatch and Utica Daily Press in the 1930s. *Courtesy Oneida County Historical Society*

LEFT: A billboard for Ballantine's ale and beer sits high atop the Devereux Block on Genesee Street in November of 1940. *Courtesy Oneida County Historical Society*

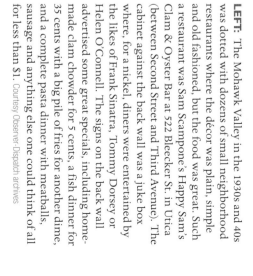

LEFT: The Mohawk Valley in the 1930s and 40s was dotted with dozens of small neighborhood restaurants where the décor was plain, simple and old fashioned, but the food was great. Such a restaurant was Sam Scampone's Happy Sam's Clam & Oyster Bar at 522 Bleecker St. in Utica (between Second Street and Third Avenue). The cabinet against the back wall was a juke box where, for a nickel, diners were entertained by the likes of Frank Sinatra, Tommy Dorsey or Helen O'Connell. The signs on the back wall advertised some great specials, including home-made clam chowder for 5 cents, a fish dinner for 35 cents with a big pile of fries for another dime, and a complete pasta dinner with meatballs, sausage and anything else one could think of all for less than $1. *Courtesy Observer-Dispatch archives*

ABOVE: Lunch counter inside the Boston Store on Genesee Street in Utica, October 1942. *Courtesy Oneida County Historical Society*

LEFT: The first Chevrolet dealership in Utica, in 1922. *Courtesy Joseph Cooper*

OPPOSITE: Modern washers and ironers on display in front of Schorer and Reardon in Utica, circa 1940. *Courtesy Oneida County Historical Society*

ABOVE: Graffenburg Dairy delivered milk with this horse-drawn wagon, 1944. The horses knew all the stops. Here they are at the 1500 block of Brinckerhoff Avenue in Utica. Roosevelt School is in the background. Courtesy Bob Rowe

RIGHT TOP: Fred F. Collis' first service truck, Utica, 1946.
Courtesy Fred F. Collis & Sons

RIGHT BOTTOM: Kraft cheese display inside a Utica grocery store, May 1947. Courtesy Oneida County Historical Society

LEFT: Interior of Pelletier Grocery Store on Kossuth Avenue, Utica, early 1930s. In the photo are Michael Nole, middle, and Margaret Pelletier, right. Courtesy Sandra Ferro

BELOW: After World War II ended in 1945, bowling became one of the most popular sports in the area. Most establishments had waiting lists for teams eager to join a league. One of the busiest places was Tex's in the 600 block of Bleecker Street (where the Sons of Italy is today). The six-lane center is shown here in 1951, just before its neighbor, Markson's Furniture Store, bought the property from Frank (Tex) Fragetta for $19,000. Bowling alleys dotted the area, including in Utica: the Palace on Lafayette Street owned by Sam Furcinito, the Empire Bowling Academy on Lafayette with Harry Rafis, the Rogers on Bleecker Street, the Heintz on Green Street owned by Joseph Heintz, the Royal on South Street with Julius and Ray Gimelli and the Sunset on Sunset Avenue managed by Frank Helmes. There also were alleys in the Knights of Columbus building, the B&D Grill in Whitesboro, Orchard Hall in Sauquoit and the Yorkville Bowling Center. Courtesy Observer-Dispatch archives

ABOVE: Utica Mutual Insurance Company's new building on Genesee Street in New Hartford, 1954. In 1959, the driver of a tractor trailer lost control on Route 12 and smashed into the front of the building. The driver was the only one killed in this accident. Courtesy Oneida County Historical Society

LEFT: The Harry Heiman showroom on Lafayette Street was open after dark to serve working customers, Utica, 1953. Courtesy Oneida County Historical Society

ABOVE: The parking lot was filled to overflowing when the new P&C supermarket opened on Campion Road in New Hartford in September of 1955. Courtesy Oneida County Historical Society

RIGHT: Shoppers take in all the specials during the grand opening of the P&C store on Campion Road in New Hartford, September 1955. Courtesy Oneida County Historical Society

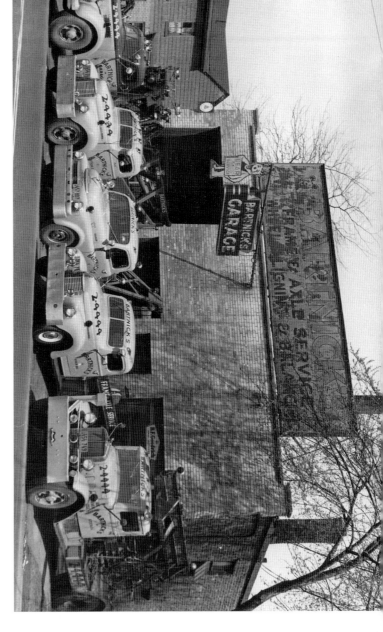

LEFT: Fleet of tow trucks and pickups belonging to Bartnick's Garage on Oriskany Street West, Utica, 1955. This location is where the North-South Arterial crosses Oriskany Street now. *Courtesy Bartnick's Garage*

BOTTOM LEFT: The record department inside Woolworth's in Utica, May 25, 1958, shows some of the popular artists of the time period including Pat Boone, Johnny Mathis and Perry Como. *Courtesy Oneida County Historical Society*

BELOW: General Electric plant on Bleecker Street in Utica, 1950s. *Courtesy Pat Caruso*

Chapter Five

INDUSTRY

I t is no secret that industry played an important role in the rapid growth of the Mohawk Valley region in the 19th century. By 1850, no region west of Albany had as many manufacturing plants.

From the 1840s to the 1950s, the region was dominated by two major industries: agriculture and textiles.

Agriculture today continues to contribute millions of dollars annually to the region's economy. The majority of jobs in the textile industry – and many other manufacturing jobs, too – have been replaced by service jobs.

But for many decades, dozens of manufacturing plants were built and prospered in the region.

Textile mills for decades made everything from knit underwear to sweaters to caps to ready-made suits and coats. The mills employed thousands of men and women and provided jobs for many of the immigrants who made the region their home at the turn of the 20th century.

But throughout the 19th and most of the 20th centuries, there were more than textiles mills in the area. A variety of goods were manufactured: beds and bed springs, guns, furniture, heating equipment and air conditioners, washing machines, automobiles, copper products, silverware and sports equipment. And much more.

When most of the textile mills began to move south after World War II ended in 1945, the region gained national fame when its civic and political leaders put into action a plan to attract new industries.

They were successful and during that "loom-to-boom" era companies such as General Electric, Bendix Aviation, Sperry UNIVAC and Chicago Pneumatic Tool and others made the region their home.

Most of those industries are gone now and the region is dominated by service jobs — jobs that are health-related and in banking, education, insurance, restaurants, tourism, amusement, recreation, etc.

But, companies such as ConMed, PAR Technology and Remington Arms continue to keep the manufacturing light burning brightly in the region. And SUNYIT, along with officials in Utica and Rome, hope to add nanotechnology to the long list of Mohawk Valley industries in the near future.

ABOVE: This large sewing room in an area knitting mill was typical of such rooms that dotted the Mohawk Valley region in the 1890s. The textile era in the region - which had begun in the early 1840s - had reached its peak by the turn of the 20th century and textiles reigned as the area's largest manufacturing industry. Utica alone had 19 large mills employing thousands of men and women. By 1910, Utica had the two largest knit goods corporations in the world - the Utica Knitting Co. and the Frisbie-Stansfield Co. There were many other knitting mills, including the Oneita; the Avalon; Globe Woolen; Brandegee, Kincaid and Wood, and the Utica Steam and Mohawk Valley. The late Dr. Virgil C. Crisafulli, former professor of economics at Utica College and a member of its original faculty, wrote in 1977: 'Most of the knit goods companies were founded by local people with local capital. This is an important distinction from present-day trends which favor firms being acquired from outside the area with outside capital and outside management.' The region's great textile era came to an end in the early 1950s when most of the mills - by then controlled by out-of-town corporations - moved to the South. New companies moved into the area and sewing rooms were replaced by manufacturing rooms and assembly lines in such places as General Electric, Bendix Aviation, Kelsey-Hayes and Sperry Univac.
Courtesy Oneida County Historical Society

LEFT TOP: Workers pose in front of Hawley and Company Foundry in the late 1800s. Courtesy Oneida County Historical Society

LEFT BOTTOM: Sperry's Carriage Works on Canal Street in Whitesboro, late 1800s. On the wagon is the Charles Sperry family. Note the phone number is 606-A. Courtesy Whitesboro Historical Society

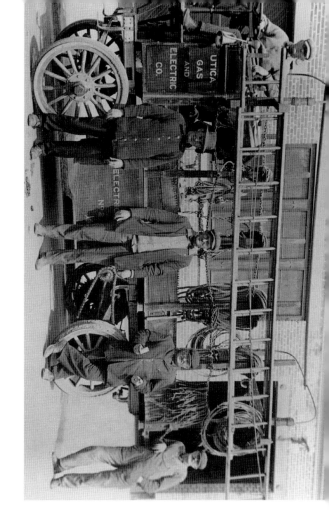

ABOVE: Linemen and a supervisor who worked for Utica Gas & Electric Co., circa 1906. *Courtesy Charles A. Carl*

BELOW: The Yetman Transmitting Typewriter Factory in Ilion, circa 1910. *Courtesy Mel and Evelyn Edwards*

ABOVE: Utica Gas & Electric Co. employees in front of the first chain-driven line truck, 1906. Charles E. 'Chubby' Walz was the driver. Photo taken on Lafayette Street in Utica. *Courtesy Charles A. Carl*

BELOW: Earl Green (foreman), Frank Gardner, Frank Flo, Stuart Darling, Jack Whyo, Winnifred Visser, Nellie Joslin and Malinda Pampby in the Anchor Knitting Mills in the old Oneida Institute Building on Main Street, Whitesboro, 1915. *Courtesy Whitesboro Historical Society*

RIGHT: The Burrstone Mill in New York Mills, circa 1915.

Courtesy Mel and Evelyn Edwards

BELOW: New York Mills workers were thrown out of their company-owned homes after they went on strike in July, 1916. On Labor Day, mill workers marched through Utica asking residents if they stood by the workers or by the company.

Courtesy Observer-Dispatch archives

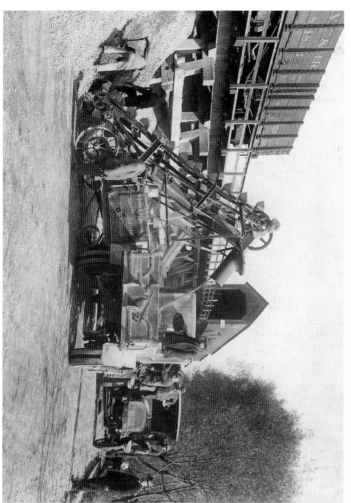

LEFT: Oneida Community Ltd. in Sherrill, circa 1920. This company was born out of the old Oneida Community, a religious and social society founded in Oneida in 1848 by John Humphrey Noyes and his followers. The Oneida Community canned fruits and vegetables, made traps and chains, made traveling bags and straw hats and mop sticks and sewing silk and, last of all, they learned how to make silver knives, forks and spoons. This was the beginning of what became Oneida Silversmiths and later the Oneida Ltd. *Courtesy Oneida County Historical Society*

BELOW: Ralph and Howard Davies and their brother-in-law, Albert Townsend, moving bags of feed from the railroad to the Lincoln Davies feed barn in Paris Station, 1922. *Courtesy Max Townsend*

LEFT: Employees of McQuade & Bannigan, Masons and Supplies at work in Utica, circa 1925. The only one identified is Arthur F. Dellenger, right side, hanging on to the truck. *Courtesy Laura Perkins*

53

RIGHT: Delivery truck owned by Andrew and Joseph Talarico, circa 1929. The two brothers were partners in the Utica trucking company.
Courtesy Ronald Talarico

BOTTOM RIGHT: Truck loaded with beans picked by workers brought to the fields in buses.
Courtesy Mary Anne Alam Hughes

BELOW: Struch Coal car, Utica, circa 1935.
Courtesy Mary Anne Alam Hughes

ABOVE: Miller Electric Company executives pose with a new washing machine in 1945 in their store on Hopper Street in Utica. From left: Bill Lorey, Fred Pidgeon, Clarence Miller, Grover Miller, Henry Miller and Edmund Conant. *Courtesy Oneida County Historical Society*

ABOVE: Women working at Divine Brothers in Utica during World War II. *Courtesy Oneida County Historical Society*

LEFT TOP: Frank Ferro, right, employee of Savage Arms, Utica, circa 1942. The company was organized in 1894 by Arthur Savage in Utica. Arthur invented the first 'hammerless' lever action rifle with the entire mechanism enclosed in a steel receiver. During World War II, Savage manufactured millions of firearms to the war effort, converting its factories to accommodate heavy munitions. *Courtesy Sandra Ferro*

BELOW: Female workers at Savage Arms during World War II. *Courtesy Oneida County Historical Society*

ABOVE: Durr's meat packing company east of the Barnes Avenue overpass, north of the New York Central tracks in 1947. *Courtesy Oneida County Historical Society*

BELOW: Talarico Brothers moving truck, circa 1948. Andrew and Joseph Talarico were partners in this local moving and excavation company. *Courtesy Ronald Talarico*

ABOVE: John Rodziewick, left, and unidentified helper loading blanks into die press at Bossert's in Utica, 1940s. *Courtesy Patricia Billings*

ABOVE: George Abel and children on Ford 10/20 tractor on the Abel farm in Coleman Mills, Town of Whitestown, 1949. From left: William, age 6; Betty, age 3; George, Sr.; George, Jr. age 9. *Courtesy George Abel*

RIGHT TOP: One of the first balers in the Paris Station area was used by the Lincoln Davies grandchildren in 1946. *Courtesy Max Townsend*

RIGHT BOTTOM: Sandy Ferro and Joan Nole in Ace Bean Lots picking beans for 50 cents a bushel in Westmoreland, 1951. *Courtesy Sandra Ferro*

RIGHT: The new Utica Mutual Insurance Company building in New Hartford featured a cafeteria in 1953, considered a necessity with the building being so far away from many restaurants. *Courtesy Oneida County Historical Society*

BELOW: Office staff at Utica Mutual Insurance Company's new facility on Genesee Street near the junction of Route 12 and Route 5. The move into the new building in 1953 was the biggest such undertaking in Utica's history. *Courtesy Oneida County Historical Society*

RIGHT: As part of its 50th anniversary celebration, Duxbak in Utica—manufacturer of outdoor clothing—held a monthly drawing for a hunting dog. Here, company officials pose with one of the prizes in November 1955. *Courtesy Oneida County Historical Society*

ABOVE: Women working in the hook tying department of the Horrocks-Ibbotson Company. The Whitesboro Street firm in Utica began in 1812 making buckskin gloves. By the time this photo was taken in 1956 the company had developed into one of the largest manufacturers in the world of fishing tackle and other products related to outdoor life. *Courtesy Oneida County Historical Society*

TOP LEFT: Dunlop Tires Rubber Corp. plant on Whitesboro Street in Utica. These are the weavers from Section 2 night shift, November 7, 1950. *Courtesy Laura Perkins*

LEFT: Cockshutt Farm Equipment Inc. plant on Truck Route 5A in New York Mills. *Courtesy Pat Caruso*

7he public must be served and from the very beginning, it has been by the Mohawk Valley region's firefighters, law enforcement officers, doctors, nurses, teachers, bankers, city and town and village officials and so many others.

The Oneida County Historical Society has hundreds of photographs of elected officials, police officers, firefighters, court officials, post office workers and others doing their jobs. Many are included in this chapter.

There are photos of the early fire wagons which were horse-drawn. By the second decade of the 20th century, most departments in the region had motorized fire trucks.

The chapter also contains a photo of the United Service Organization's (USO) room at the southwest corner of Utica's Union Station. During World War II, from 1942 to 1945, the USO offered servicemen and women between trains a place where they could relax for an hour or two, enjoy a sandwich and cup of coffee or write a letter home – all courtesy of the USO and the more than 800 volunteers in the region who worked there.

During its 52 months of operation – it remained open after the war ended in August 1945 – nearly 235,000 men and women in the military took advantage of the USO's hospitality.

The items to keep the USO room operating – food, stationery, furniture, etc. – were all donated by volunteers and local restaurants and stores. Now that's public service!

OPPOSITE: Utica Fire Department Chief Frank P. Breitenberg with an unidentified driver in the 1920s. *Courtesy Oneida County Historical Society*

61

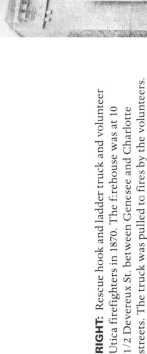

RIGHT: Rescue hook and ladder truck and volunteer Utica firefighters in 1870. The firehouse was at 10 1/2 Devereux St. between Genesee and Charlotte streets. The truck was pulled to fires by the volunteers. Courtesy Oneida County Historical Society

FAR RIGHT: A Utica police officer in the late 1800s. Courtesy Oneida County Historical Society

BOTTOM RIGHT: Waterville Fire Department in the late 1800s. Courtesy Oneida County Historical Society

BELOW: The Utica Fire Department's Engine No. 1 and combination wagon in the 1890s. On the engine are driver Frank Breitenberg, Sr. and Engineer Albright. Standing on the ground are Captain Walker, Stoker Lux and Fireman Leonard Waters. On the wagon are Driver Chamber Adams and Fireman James Monroe. Standing in front of the wagon are Fireman William Walker and Fireman Frank Brietenberg Jr., who would later become chief. Courtesy Oneida County Historical Society

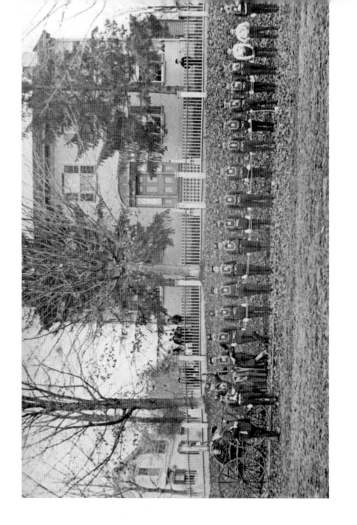

ABOVE: Faxton Hospital in Utica, circa 1905. *Courtesy Mel and Evelyn Edwards*

TOP LEFT: The apparatus at Utica Fire Department's Station 4 in the late 1890s included a hose wagon and the 1884 Clapp & Jones 2nd-class steamer. *Courtesy Oneida County Historical Society*

LEFT: In 1906, the Utica Fire Department purchased a powerful American LaFrance Metropolitan steamer and assigned it to Engine 2 company located on the east side of John Street between Bleecker and Elizabeth streets, across from St. John's Church. It took three horses to pull the Metro and it's shown here with Firefighter Frank H. Clark at the reins. The department had been using steam power since 1864, but nothing like the Metropolitan which had a steam boiler able to produce enough pressure to throw a stream of water farther than any other engine in the department. In 1917, the department became motorized and the Metro was placed in storage and eventually sold for junk. But it was never destroyed and in 1973 Abe Nathan & Sons, Utica scrap metal dealers, presented the steamer to the fire department. It was cleaned up enough to participate in the department's centennial parade in 1974. In 1995, the Utica National Insurance Group agreed to complete the restoration project and today the magnificent red, yellow and gold steamer greets visitors in the lobby of the insurance company's new building on Lafayette Street in downtown Utica. The apparatus on the right in this photo is a one-horse hose wagon and the pillared building is the old Oneida County Court House, which was built in 1852 and was replaced in 1909 by a new court house on Elizabeth Street. *Courtesy Oneida County Historical Society*

ABOVE: Utica Fire Department, Truck No. 3, 1906. William Seifer (Driver), George C. McCoy (Tillerman). Standing left to right are Captain Edward G. Miller, Lieutenant Joseph A. McInrow, Fireman Harvey Wilcox, Fireman Alex Scholl, Fireman Joseph Dwyer and Fireman Albert Moreshead. *Courtesy McCoy Family*

RIGHT TOP: During a staged demonstration by the Utica Fire Department in 1904, one of three horses pulling the No. 4 engine goes down en route to a test fire alarm in downtown Utica. As horrific as it appears in this photo, the horse actually scrambled to its feet, and, without suffering even a scratch, resumed his part in the run. Fred Groat is the driver and the event took place on Genesee Street between Catherine and Broad streets. *Courtesy Oneida County Historical Society*

RIGHT BOTTOM: Members of the Clayville Fire Department ready to participate in one of the relay events at a firemen's convention in Rome in the early 1900s. *Courtesy Oneida County Historical Society*

TOP LEFT: A view of the old city hall on Genesee Street in Utica, circa 1910.
Courtesy Mel and Evelyn Edwards

TOP RIGHT: Utica Fire Department No. 7's combination wagon in 1915. On the seat are Driver William Farrell and Captain Charles Keefe. Standing, from left, are Firemen William Jones, Joe Aigner, and George 'Tig' Jones, and Lieutenant Frank Clark.
Courtesy Oneida County Historical Society

ABOVE: Engine No. 7's Clapp & Jones steamer in 1915 with Driver Martin Bach on the seat and Engineers Arthur Groat and Frank Ellerd on the ground.
Courtesy Oneida County Historical Society

LEFT: Utica Fire Department's Truck No. 2 in front of the Central Fire Department between 1911 and 1915. The driver is William L. Richards.
Courtesy Oneida County Historical Society

LEFT TOP: Where have all the horses gone? On June 1, 1874, Utica organized a paid fire department. Its engines and trucks were pulled by horses. In July 1913, the city purchased its first pieces of motorized apparatus for the fire and police departments - a car for Fire Chief Daniel J. Sullivan, a Seagrave chemical and hose rig assigned to Engine No. 1 on Park Avenue near Oneida Square, a police patrol car and a police ambulance. As more motorized rigs were purchased, some of the horses were sold to trucking firms. One morning in October 1917, the last horses were sold at auctions, except for a team of grays which were kept in No. 1 Engine House until 1921. Utica became one of the first cities in the country to have a completely motorized fire department. The cost of its 19 motor apparatus was $110,000. To celebrate the occasion, a big civic parade was held on Saturday, October 24, to show Uticans its modern fire department. Before the parade started on Bagg's Square, the motorized rigs lined up on the north side of Broad Street between Genesee and John streets. *Courtesy Oneida County Historical Society*

LEFT BOTTOM: Utica Fire Department's No. 3 crew enjoys a game of chance in 1916. *Courtesy Oneida County Historical Society*

RIGHT: Members of the Oriskany Falls Home Defense Corps posed on the steps of the landmark stone Congregational Church during World War I. The group was organized to protect such strategic targets as local industries, bridges, etc. from German saboteurs. *Courtesy Oneida County Historical Society*

OPPOSITE: Crowds pack the Utica train depot to see off their young men headed to World War I.

RIGHT: U.S.O. lounge at Union Station in Utica, during World War II.

Courtesy Mel and Evelyn Edwards

BOTTOM RIGHT: The Home for the Homeless in Utica, circa 1920.

Courtesy Diana C. Howard

BELOW: The administration building of the Masonic Home in Utica, circa 1920.

Courtesy Diana C. Howard

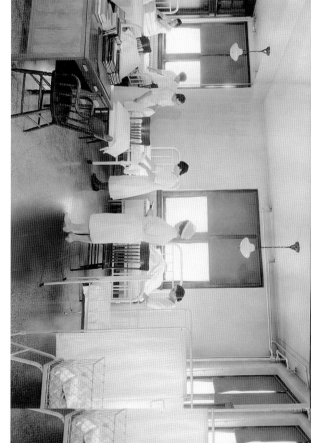

ABOVE: A class in 'Nursing Foundations' at St. Elizabeth Hospital in the 1920s. *Courtesy Observer-Dispatch archives*

TOP LEFT: Children's music room in the Masonic Home in Utica, circa 1920. *Courtesy Diana C. Howard*

LEFT: A fire engine from the Willowvale Fire Department in 1922. *Courtesy Martin Shepherd*

ABOVE: Officers and non-commissioned officers of Company L, 10th Infantry, New York National Guard, April 1923. Courtesy Oneida County Historical Society

RIGHT: Police officer Henry Looft, right, and his partner (possibly Dave), at the Shell gas station on James Street at the corner of St. Vincent Street in Utica, 1941. In the background is the former James Street bus loop. Courtesy Bob Rowe

BELOW: Utica Fire Department, Platoon No. 1, 1941. Courtesy McCoy Family

ABOVE: Utica Citizens Cadet Corps, November 2, 1943.
Courtesy Oneida County Historical Society

RIGHT: Fire personnel gather for a photo during a Fire Instructors conference in Utica, 1950. *Courtesy Pat Caruso*

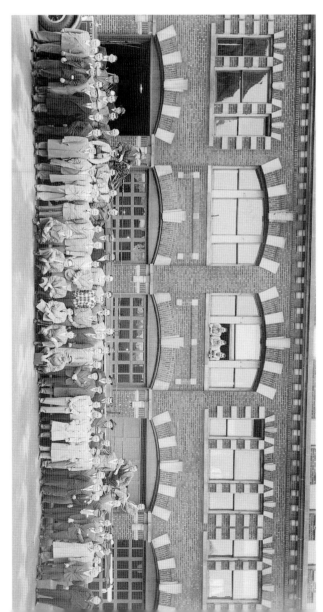

LEFT: On the afternoon of October 10, 1952, President Harry Truman's train pulled into Utica's Union Station as part of his whistle-stop tour campaigning for Democrat presidential candidate Adlai Stevenson. Truman addressed a crowd of 6,000 from the rear platform of his train, just as he had done in 1948 when his 'whistle-stop' campaign stopped in Utica - a campaign that led Truman to an upset victory over Republican Thomas E. Dewey. In his 1952 stop, he again treated his audience to his 'give-em-hell' technique when he attacked Stevenson's Republican opponent, Dwight D. Eisenhower, for his alleged 'betrayal' of Gen. George C. Marshall and Philip C. Jessup, a former Utican and graduate of Hamilton College, was ambassador-at-large in the Truman administration. Truman said Eisenhower had endorsed U.S. Sen. Joseph McCarthy for re-election 'even though the Republican senator from Wisconsin had questioned the patriotism of Marshall and Jessup,' McCarthy had been conducting a Senate investigation of what he said was Communist influence on U.S. foreign policy. In November, Eisenhower was elected 34th president of the United States. *Courtesy Observer-Dispatch archives*

Chapter Seven

RECREATION

W hen new industries began to locate in the Mohawk Valley after World War II, many of their executives who had relocated here said that one of the things that attracted them to the area was its many parks where its employees could relax and play; its many streams, rivers and lakes where they could fish; its many snow-covered hills where they could ski.

Recreational places are important to a region and Mohawk Valley has been blessed with many such places through the years.

Photos in this chapter show men, women and youngsters taking advantage of the many recreational opportunities in the region — from Little League play to circuses to band concerts to fairs and much more.

There are dozens of such places to play and relax in the region, led by two recreational giants: Sylvan Beach and the Central Adirondacks.

Years ago, bicycle racing was all the rage. So was professional baseball when both Little Falls and Utica

fielded teams in the New York-Penn League. Some of their players went on to the major leagues.

And in the 1940s, the Utica Blue Sox were the talk of the town when many of its players became all-stars in the big leagues, including Richie Ashburn (a Hall of Famer), Granny Hamner, Stan Lopata and Billy Glynn.

Softball and bowling have been popular in the region for years as well.

And today one can enjoy the many high school sports teams in action, top-notch college teams at play, shows at Utica's Stanley Center for the Arts and Rome's Capitol Theater. And let's not forget the many amateur theater groups, such The Players of Utica.

After a hard day's work or hours in the classroom, residents look for a place to relax. Maria and Thomas Proctor gave the city of Utica hundreds of acres of land for its park system at the turn of the 20th century. The Proctors believed that citizens had to have parks and playgrounds where they could unwind and enjoy life.

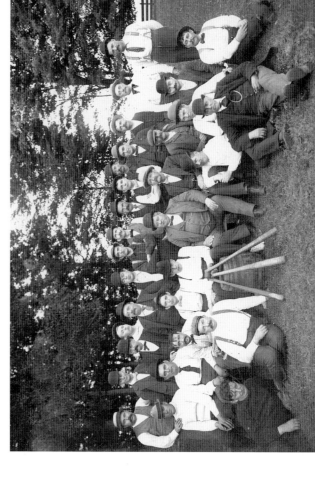

ABOVE: An 1890s circus parade in Downtown Utica on Genesee St. looking south to Columbia St. The store with the Butterfield awning in the center of the photo is where the Radisson Hotel-Utica Centre is today. *Courtesy Oneida County Historical Society*

BELOW: West Utica Outing Club, September 11, 1892. *Courtesy Oneida County Historical Society*

ABOVE: A circus parade at the foot of Genesee Street near train station, Utica, 1885. *Courtesy Ann Penberthy Allen*

TOP: Penny-Farthing bicycle race in 1889 at the Utica Driving Park (today the site is occupied by the Masonic Home on Utica's eastern boundary). Participants were part of an organized group who held meetings and had periodic races. *Courtesy Ann Penberthy Allen*

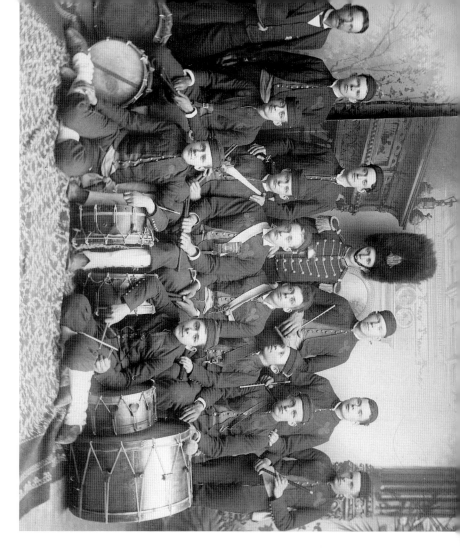

ABOVE: Yorkville Military Band in the early 1900s. *Courtesy Oneida County Historical Society*

LEFT: Canton Utica No. 23, P. M. Drum Corps, May 30, 1890. Front row, from left: D. L. Winston, Fred Groat. Second row, from left: G. O. Carter, M. V. Gorton, W. T. Carter, George Eastman, C. F. Smith, D. A. Carter Jr. Back row, from left: D. A. Carter, director; K. B. Smith, F. C. Carter, H. C. Smaltz, John Herbig, G. F. Teale, J. Hughes. *Courtesy Oneida County Historical Society*

RIGHT: One of the most popular attractions at the Utica Park from the day it first opened in 1891 was the Franz Rath Orchestra. The band not only provided music for dancing, but also presented concerts during summer evenings. The park - located at the eastern end of Bleecker Street just east of Masonic Home - featured a zoo, large flower gardens, picnic grounds, a baseball diamond, a half-mile track for bicycle races, amusement rides that included a roller coaster and merry-go-round and restaurants big and small. The Rath orchestra, shown here on Sept. 19, 1903, included from left: Jules Russ, Henry Gliffe, August Bernholdt, Mr. and Mrs. Ben Rolfe, James Henry (Harry) McCormick, Franz and Rosa Rath, unknown, Lucy McCormick, unknown, John Rath and John Albrecht. The park, which had been built by Utica's trolley company with tracks leading to the park's front entrance, flourished until automobiles appeared on the scene with the ability to take people to faraway recreation areas. In 1925, the park was renamed Forest Park. In 1934, it closed, although some groups used it for clambakes in the 1940s. *Courtesy Oneida County Historical Society*

ABOVE: Boat house on Oriskany Creek in Summit Park in Oriskany, circa 1907. *Courtesy Diana C. Howard*

LEFT: Utica Gas & Electric Co. picnic for employees and their families at Trenton Falls, circa 1906. *Courtesy Charles A. Carl*

LEFT: Utica Park, circa 1905. *Courtesy Mel and Evelyn Edwards*

OPPOSITE: Bayne Camp No. 31 Sons of Veterans band, New York Mills, circa 1900. *Courtesy Oneida County Historical Society*

RIGHT: The Balloon Farm in Frankfort, circa 1907. The mansion at left was purchased in 1889 by famed balloon enthusiasts Carl and Mary Myers. Mary was better known as Carlotta, the Lady Aeronaut, the name she performed under at fairs and expositions. *Courtesy Mel and Evelyn Edwards*

BOTTOM RIGHT: Oneida County Fair, Rome. *Courtesy Oneida County Historical Society*

BELOW: A. D. H. ball team clambake in Clinton, September 15, 1912. *Courtesy Oneida County Historical Society*

ABOVE: Ralph Davie, left, and family dressed up for the Paris Hill Fair in the town of Paris in 1927. *Courtesy Max Townsend*

LEFT: A family enjoys cotton candy at a Ringling Brothers Circus parade in Utica.

Courtesy Oneida County Historical Society

LEFT: Out for a ride in the soft fluffy snow in back of Lincoln Davies Store in Paris Station, 1931.

Courtesy Max Townsend

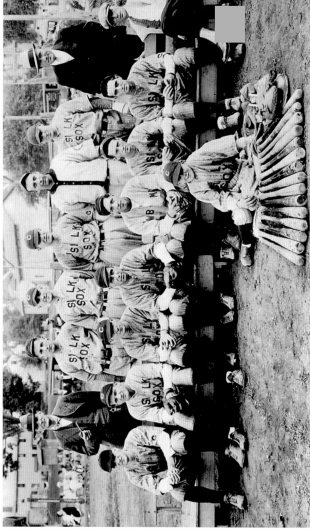

ABOVE: The Chadwicks Silk Sox Baseball Team in 1932. *Courtesy Evelyn Edwards*

BELOW: The Utica Braves baseball team, 1940. This team took fourth place in the Can-Am League. *Courtesy June Taylor*

ABOVE: Foster Bros. baseball team, circa 1915. In the photo are Charles J. Ritzel, Sr., back row far right; John Ritzel, back row, second from right; Charlie Whitney, back row, third from right. Foster Bros. was a bedding company on Broad Street in Utica. *Courtesy Gerard Ritzel*

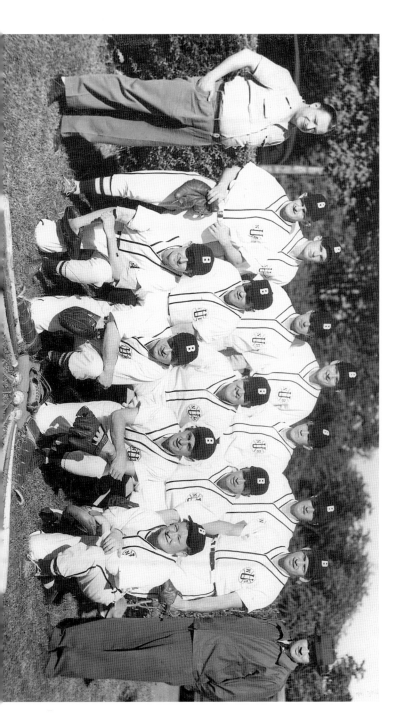

ABOVE: The 1941 Utica Braves baseball team in the Can-Am League.
Courtesy Oneida County Historical Society

LEFT: The North Utica Boosters in 1946.
Courtesy Observer-Dispatch archives

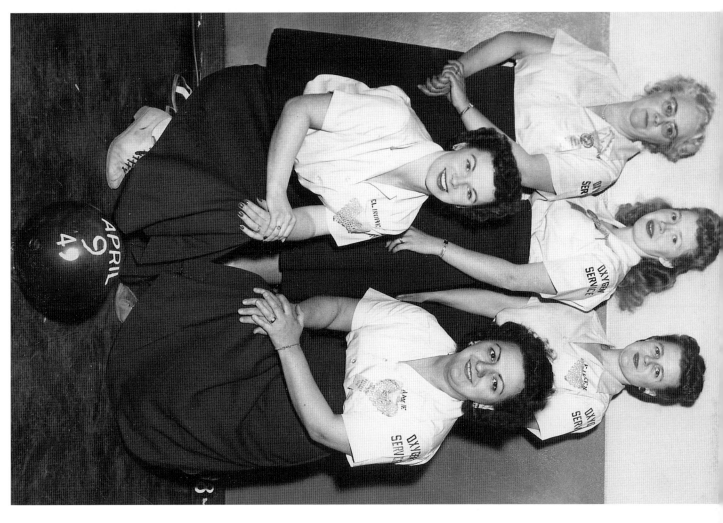

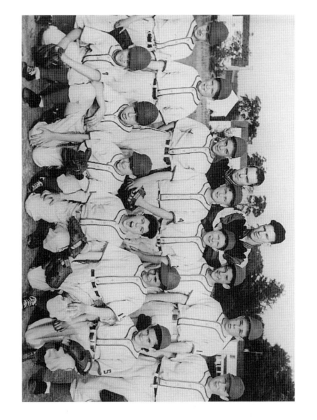

ABOVE: The North Utica Athletic Association Football team in 1950.
Courtesy James Gaffney

LEFT: Oxygen Service women's bowling team, April 9, 1949.
Courtesy Oneida County Historical Society

OPPOSITE: The John T. Buckley swimming pool at Albany Street, Culver Avenue and Welshbush Road was added to T. R. Proctor Park by the Works Progress Administration and became a haven for East Utica youngsters during the summer. Photo taken June 20, 1944. *Courtesy Oneida County Historical Society*

BELOW: South Utica Little League team, circa 1951 (the first year of Little League in South Utica). Included in the photo are Steve Wynn (of Las Vegas fame), Mike Slive (now commissioner of the Southeastern Athletic Conference and the former BCS commission chief executive).
Courtesy Observer-Dispatch archives

RIGHT: St. Anthony Catholic Youth Organization Basketball team, circa 1952. Courtesy Nick Piperata

BELOW: Synchronized swim show at YWCA in Utica, 1954. Swimmers are Mitzi Bankratz, JoAnn Mursh, Mildred Ryan and Fran Lemuzza. Courtesy Diane Lange

ABOVE: Sunset Majors Bowling League members, Utica, 1950s. Frank Ferro was one of the members. Courtesy Sandra Ferro

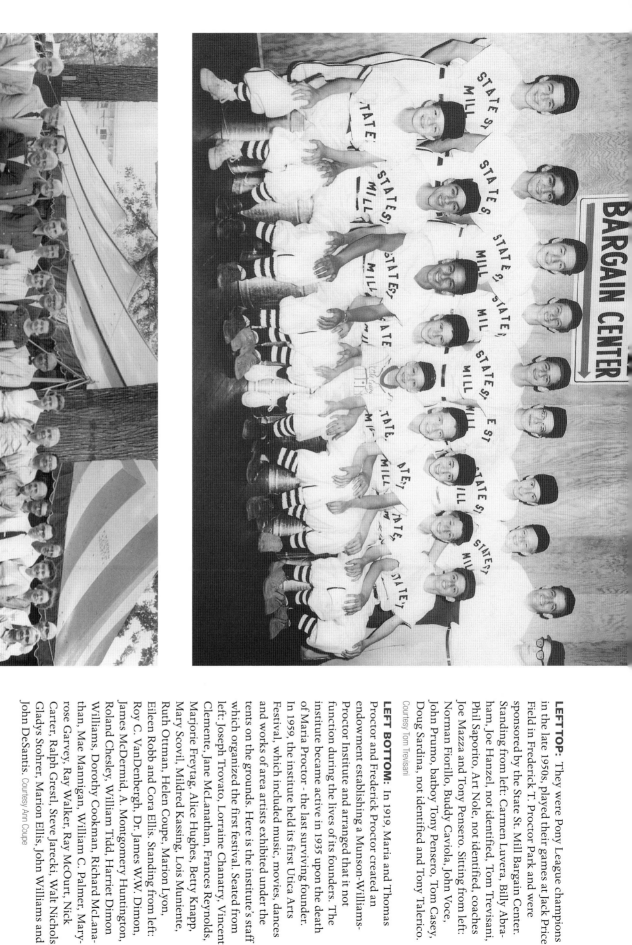

LEFT TOP: They were Pony League champions in the late 1950s, played their games at Jack Price Field in Frederick T. Proctor Park and were sponsored by the State St. Mill Bargain Center. Standing from left: Carmen Luvera, Billy Abraham, Joe Hanzel, not identified, Tom Trevisani, Phil Saporito, Art Nole, not identified, coaches Joe Mazza and Tony Pensero. Sitting from left: Norman Fiorillo, Buddy Caviola, John Voce, John Prumo, batboy Tony Pensero, Tom Casey, Doug Sardina, not identified and Tony Talerico. *Courtesy Tom Trevisani*

LEFT BOTTOM: In 1919, Maria and Thomas Proctor and Frederick Proctor created an endowment establishing a Munson-Williams-Proctor Institute and arranged that it not function during the lives of its founders. The institute became active in 1935 upon the death of Maria Proctor - the last surviving founder. In 1959, the institute held its first Utica Arts Festival, which included music, movies, dances and works of area artists exhibited under the tents on the grounds. Here is the institute's staff which organized the first festival. Seated from left: Joseph Trovato, Lorraine Chanatry, Vincent Clemente, Jane McLanathan, Frances Reynolds, Marjorie Freytag, Alice Hughes, Betty Knapp, Mary Scovil, Mildred Kassing, Lois Muniente, Ruth Ottman, Helen Coupe, Marion Lyon. Eileen Robb and Cora Ellis. Standing from left: Roy C. VanDenbergh, Dr. James W.W. Dimon, James McDermid, A. Montgomery Huntington, Roland Chesley, William Tidd, Harriet Dimon Williams, Dorothy Cookman, Richard McLanathan, Mae Mannigan, William C. Palmer, Maryrose Garvey, Ray Walker, Ray McOurt, Nick Carter, Ralph Grestl, Steve Jarecki, Walt Nichols, Gladys Stohrer, Marion Ellis, John Williams and John DeSantis. *Courtesy Ann Coupe*

Chapter Eight

COMMUNITY

7his chapter could be titled "Family Album," for many of its photos come right from the album that Mom, Dad, Uncle Joe, Aunt Bea and Grandma and Grandpa carefully kept through the years – a record of family members, homes, and activities.

There are photos of servicemen and women returning home from war, those taken at church weddings, the family on the farm and much more.

Communities have much in common, whether it be Bridgewater or Ilion or Boonville or wherever. They have their churches, schools, clubs, organizations, restaurants, grocery stores, supermarkets, bakeries, taverns, etc. And every community has its gem or two – a historic

site, a popular park, a monument.

One photo in this chapter depicts Fountain Elms on the Munson-Williams-Proctor Institute campus. The Victorian-era house museum is one of Utica's gems, but really belongs to every community in the region.

It was established in 1919 by Maria, Thomas and Frederick Proctor and Otto Meyer to "share with their community the pleasures and advantages of artistic and cultural activities." The region has benefitted from their gift ever since.

And, of course, a community is made up of people and it is the "family album faces" that make this chapter come alive.

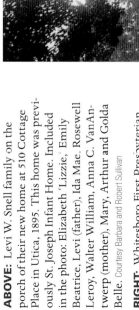

ABOVE: Levi W. Snell family on the porch of their new home at 510 Cottage Place in Utica, 1895. This home was previously St. Joseph Infant Home. Included in the photo: Elizabeth 'Lizzie,' Emily Beatrice, Levi (father), Ida Mae. Rosewell Leroy, Walter William, Anna C. VanAntwerp (mother), Mary, Arthur and Golda Belle. *Courtesy Barbara and Robert Sullivan*

RIGHT: Whitesboro First Presbyterian Church on Main Street in Whitesboro, early 1900s. *Courtesy Whitesboro Historical Society*

ABOVE: The country home of Minnie Stewart in Clinton, early 1900s. In the photo are Minnie Stewart, Robert Stewart, Arch Stewart and Wessell Doughtry. *Courtesy Laura Perkins*

BELOW: Hart summer home on Clinton Street, Whitesboro. This Southern Plantation house burned in 1904 and was rebuilt in 1946. It became Plantation Restaurant and later Hart's Hill Inn. *Courtesy Whitesboro Historical Society*

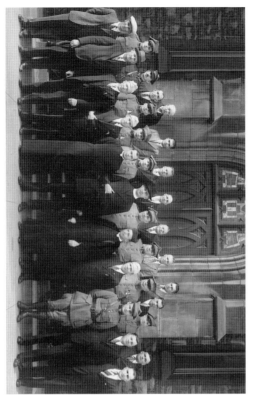

ABOVE: Priests and soldiers dressed in Polish military uniforms in front of Holy Trinity Church on Lincoln Avenue, Utica, circa 1920. Several are wearing hats worn by officers of the Polish Army in France. *Courtesy Laura Perkins*

LEFT: The honorable James S. Sherman of Utica served as vice president of the United States from March 4, 1909, until his death, October 30, 1912. Sherman's photo is inset over an image of his residence in Utica. *Courtesy Mel and Evelyn Edwards*

BELOW: Family of Lincoln Davies, Paris Station, 1922. From left: Hazel, Florence, Louise and Mother May Davies (Lincoln's wife). Sitting, from left: Ralph, Howard and Dr. Stanley Davies. *Courtesy Max Townsend*

ABOVE: Stanley Swalgin, grandfather of Patricia Billings, at a farm in Waterville, 1930. *Courtesy Patricia Billings*

RIGHT: June Williams, age 7, and Joan Repple, age 1, in front of the Williams home at 1410 Dudley Avenue, Utica, 1940. The home is no longer standing. *Courtesy June Taylor*

BOTTOM LEFT: Members of Society Sicignanese gather at Hotel Martin in Utica to celebrate their 25th anniversary on September 22, 1935. *Courtesy Laura Perkins*

RIGHT: Williams family in front of their home at 1410 Dudley Avenue, Utica, 1940. In the photo are: Marvin, Florence, Jane, George, Jack and June. *Courtesy June Taylor*

ABOVE: Art Repple, of Utica, served in the Navy from 1943 to 1946. *Courtesy June Taylor*

RIGHT TOP: James Collis sitting on his father's oil truck, Utica, 1942. *Courtesy Fred F. Collis & Sons*

RIGHT BOTTOM: Marvin Williams served in the Navy from 1943 to 1946. Photo taken in front of the home at 1410 Dudley Avenue in Utica. The house is no longer standing. *Courtesy June Taylor*

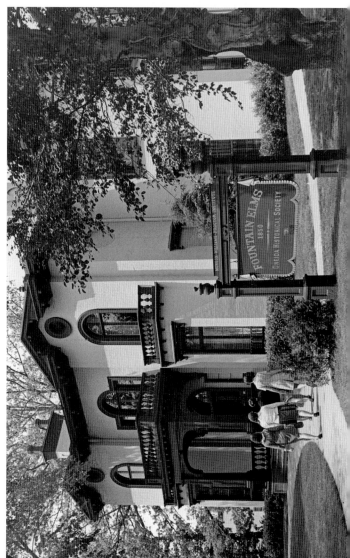

RIGHT: Daughters of Union Veterans of Civil War putting a wreath on Soldier's and Sailor's monument on Oneida Square during Memorial Day activities in Utica, circa 1949. Courtesy McCoy Family

BOTTOM RIGHT: Elaine Roberts, age 12, (front center), Janet Roach, age 12, (on left), June Williams, age 12, (on right), and Cynthia Ructer, age 15 (in back) at Johnson Park in Utica. Courtesy June Taylor

BELOW: Fountain Elms historic home in Utica. Original construction was completed in 1852 with remodeling and additions occurring into the early and late 20th century. Courtesy Oneida County Historical Society

ABOVE: Women dressed for what is believed to be a Mardi Gras party at Blessed Sacrament Church auditorium, Utica, 1952. Included in the photo are: Betty Alessandrini, Leula Caramadre, Mini Giglotti, Marie Ciolla, Adeline Gutowski, Sandy Ferro, Joan Roth and Anita Fiacano. *Courtesy Sandra Ferro*

TOP LEFT: Brownies have a photo taken for Communion Breakfast at Blessed Sacrament Church in Utica, 1951. Ruth Mundshenk, Brownie leader, on left. *Courtesy Sandra Ferro*

LEFT: Albert Pfistorer, milkman for Hameline's Dairy in Utica, 1955. Pfistorer's house on Lenox Avenue is in the background. *Courtesy Michelle Jones*

RIGHT: Birthday party for Betty Abel, age 4, 1950. The party was at the Abel Farm in Coleman Mills, Town of Whitestown. Abel children, from left: George, age 9; Betty, age 4; William, age 7. *Courtesy George Abel*

BOTTOM LEFT: Three servicemen from Utica, George Williams (just out of the Army) Paul Mason (soon to leave the Navy) and John Williams (soon to leave the military). Photo was taken in 1953. *Courtesy June Taylor*

BOTTOM RIGHT: Out for a drive in an automobile in the 1950s, are Gail Corabi (on top of car) and Ursala Leo Grande. The other person is unidentified. They are near the Power Dam in New Hartford. *Courtesy Diane Langelor*

ABOVE: Bethesda Congregational Church on Washington Street, below Westminster Presbyterian Church. It was built in 1872 and demolished for Urban Renewal in 1962. This is the current site of Radisson Hotel – Utica Center. *Courtesy Gilbert H. Jones*

RIGHT: Holy Trinity (Russian Orthodox) Monastery soon after it was erected in Jordanville, 1950. After this photo was taken, the monastery was decorated with frescos inside and out. Over the years trees have grown up on every side of the monastery and this view can never be replicated. *Courtesy Jerome F. Weber*

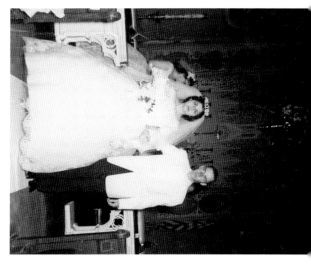

LEFT: Mary Anne Alam Hughes and Thomas Robert Hughes on their wedding day, April 18, 1959. The wedding was at Our Lady of Lourdes Church (the old structure). A new church was constructed in the late 1960s and the old one torn down. *Courtesy Mary Anne Alam Hughes*

Chapter Nine

DISASTERS

Every region in the country has had its disasters and the Mohawk Valley is no exception.

This chapter contains many photos of fires through the years that have taken lives and caused millions of dollars in damage.

There also are photos of the Great Flood in Herkimer in 1910. In late February, ice jams formed where West Canada Creek enters the Mohawk River. On February 28, the creek overflowed and its water headed for the village of Herkimer. The result: some sections of the vil-

lage were under three feet of water. Electric trolley cars were stopped in their tracks and could not move. Many houses were knocked off their foundations. Dynamite was used to break up the ice jam. Flood damage caused hundreds of thousands of dollars in damage.

Through the years, too, many area residents have lost their lives or been injured in fierce snowstorms. And the region has had more than its share of train wrecks, including the one in Little Falls in 1940 that took 31 lives.

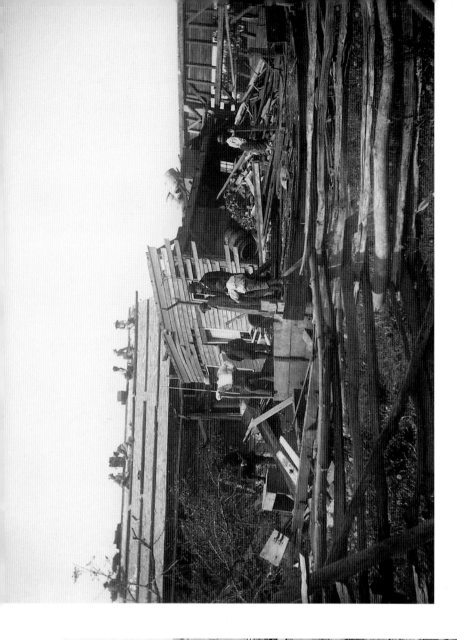

ABOVE: Flooding near Albany Street in Utica in the late 1800s. Courtesy Oneida County Historical Society

RIGHT TOP: Aftermath of the cyclone that hit Westmoreland June 3, 1897. Courtesy Oneida County Historical Society

RIGHT BOTTOM: The YMCA building in Utica after it was destroyed by fire March 1, 1907. Courtesy Mel and Evelyn Edwards

LEFT TOP AND BOTTOM: A mistake by a telegrapher in Lyons Falls early on a Saturday morning on July 4, 1908, resulted in one of the worst train wrecks ever in the Boonville area. Six people were killed and 10 injured when the northbound Thousand Islands Flyer passenger train and a southbound freight train collided head-on just north of Boonville on the single-track Black River rail line. This photo shows a steam crane, on the left, clearing the wreckage later in the day. The Flyer had wired the operator in Lyons Falls that it would wait in Boonville until 5:15 for the freight train to go by. The operator wired the information to the engineer of the freight train, but mistakenly said that the Flyer would wait until 5:55 instead of 5:15. The freight train engineer figured he could easily reach Boonville by 5:55. At 5:15, the Flyer pulled out of Boonville and proceeded north. At 5:30, the trains collided. The dead included Albert Reiber and Stephen O'Brien, both from Utica and both engine men on the Flyer, and Andrew Hageman, of Utica, brakeman on the freight train. Also killed were two firemen on the Flyer and one if its passengers. Most of the injured were from Utica. Courtesy Oneida County Historical Society

ABOVE: A train wreck on the New York Central tracks between Rome and Oriskany, April 8, 1910. *Courtesy Oneida County Historical Society*

RIGHT: School children in front of the burned out remains of Utica Free Academy, April 27, 1908.
Courtesy Mel and Evelyn Edwards

BELOW: The ruins of Utica Free Academy, April 1908.
Courtesy Mel and Evelyn Edwards

ABOVE: Herkimer citizens survey the damage during the great flood of 1910.
Courtesy Mel and Evelyn Edwards

TOP LEFT: Steuben Street in Herkimer strewn with debris and ice chunks after the disastrous flooding in March of 1910.
Courtesy Mel and Evelyn Edwards

LEFT: Main Street in Herkimer during the great flood of 1910.
Courtesy Mel and Evelyn Edwards

ABOVE: Winters continue to be cold and snowy, but powerful plows and plenty of salt and other concoctions keep roads bare most of the time. Not so in the 1930s and 40s when the snows usually arrived in early November and stayed around until late March, making the good old days not so good for motorists. Here is a car slowly moving along one of Utica's side streets. Roads were packed with snow all winter since they were not salted. Homes' coal-burning furnaces, however, produced tons of ashes. Homeowners placed the ashes in receptacles and each week city trucks picked them up at curbside and spread the ashes along intersections to alleviate slippery conditions there. *Courtesy Observer-Dispatch archives*

ABOVE: High winds from the southwest took the roof off part of the Marshal milk plant and ice house at Paris Station in 1930. Part of the roof was found in a farm yard about a mile away. *Courtesy Max Townsend*

TOP LEFT: Flood waters washed away the Cooper Street bridge, Oriskany Falls, June 11, 1917. *Courtesy Oneida County Historical Society*

RIGHT: Stores flooded in Utica, circa 1930. *Courtesy Mary Anne Alam Hughes*

ABOVE: Paris Station farmers and neighbors shoveling trenches to loosen the snow alongside the city's snow plow, 1941. *Courtesy Max Townsend*

TOP LEFT: John Williams shoveling snow after a heavy snowfall in Utica, 1940. *Courtesy June Taylor*

LEFT: Pedestrians try to get around Utica after a heavy snowfall in 1940. *Courtesy June Taylor*

ABOVE: Winds reaching 75 miles an hour and gusting to 90 miles an hour swept through Oneida County on November 25, 1950, uprooting trees, disrupting power and telephone service and blowing pedestrians off their feet. Damage reached tens of thousands of dollars. This photo shows the Utica Municipal Airport on River Road in Marcy, where winds ripped up a small section of the roof on one of the hangars. Officials at the Civil Aeronautics Administration (CAA) station there said that winds persisted at 60 to 75 miles an hour. Much of the CAA equipment had been moved earlier in the week to the new Oneida County Airport in Oriskany.
Courtesy Observer-Dispatch archives

LEFT: A view of Boonville after the big snow storm of 1943.
Courtesy Oneida County Historical Society

OPPOSITE: A Utica fire engine sits on Genesee Street January 31, 1948 after a large fire ripped through the block the night before. Many local businesses were damaged. Seventeen firefighter were injured including nine who were badly burned. *Courtesy Oneida County Historical Society*

BELOW: Fire at Utica Structural Steel, November 5, 1952.
Courtesy Oneida County Historical Society

Chapter Ten

CELEBRATIONS

esidents of the Mohawk Valley have had much to celebrate through the years – centennials, sesquicentennials, bicentennials galore since communities were permanently established in the region in times before the Revolutionary War.

Those are big celebrations, but let's not forget the others such as weddings, birthdays, anniversaries, etc.

Of course, what's a celebration without a parade and the region has shown that it loves a parade.

In August 1908, the entire region proudly marched to band music to honor Utica's James Schoolcraft Sherman who had been nominated to run for vice president of the United States on the Republican ticket headed by William Howard Taft. And there was more celebrating in

November 1908 when they won.

In 1932, the region joined Utica in celebrating its 100th anniversary as a city. In 1832, it had become only the sixth city in New York state – after New York City, Albany, Schenectady, Troy and Hudson.

Every community celebrated the end of World War II in August 1945 when Japan unconditionally surrendered to the United States and its Allies.

There will always be wonderful celebrations as long as we have St. Patrick's Day, Memorial Day, Veterans Day, the Boilermaker Road Race and the Fourth of July.

And there will always be hundreds of people taking photos of those events. That's what made this chapter possible.

ABOVE: New Hartford centennial celebration in 1888.
Courtesy Oneida County Historical Society

TOP RIGHT: Clinton, NY parade, circa 1905.
Courtesy Oneida County Historical Society

RIGHT: Roberts Parry & Co., hardware and stoves delivery wagon in front of the business in Utica, early 1900. The wagon is decorated for a parade or celebration. Courtesy Laura Perkins

ABOVE: The village of Herkimer celebrated its 100th anniversary in 1907 and the highlight of its centennial celebration was the unveiling in Myers Park of a statue of Gen. Nicholas Herkimer, sculpted by Burr Miller and depicting the wounded general at the Battle of Oriskany during the Revolutionary War, urging his American militiamen to fight on. The base of the sculpture is a 25-ton boulder that was found on a farm near Remsen. This photo shows men lifting the boulder onto a railroad flat car that would take it to Herkimer.

Courtesy Observer-Dispatch archives

ABOVE: The Conkling Unconditionals in their unmistakable white uniforms march past the Soldiers and Sailors Monument as they escort the honorable James S. Sherman home from a Western trip, October 10, 1908. *Courtesy Mel and Evelyn Edwards*

LEFT: In 1908, Thomas and Maria Williams Proctor and Frederick and Rachel Williams Proctor gave the city of Utica hundreds of acres for its public park system. On Saturday, July 8, 1916, Uticans said 'thank you' by organizing the first Proctor Day celebration. Thousands of people - most of them carrying American flags - paraded to four of the parks given to the city by the Proctors - Horatio Seymour Park at Sunset Avenue and Burrstone Road, Watson-Williams Park on James Street, Frederick T. Proctor Park on Culver Avenue and Rutger Street and Roscoe Conkling Park on the Parkway (shown in this photo). There also was a program by children on the lawn of the House of Good Shepherd on Genesee Street, built and donated by the Proctors in 1904. It was a thrilling outburst of love from the people to the Proctors and the day was filled with picnics on the parks, band concerts, dances, singing, games and aeroplane demonstrations. Thomas Proctor spoke at Conkling Park and said: ' On behalf of my wife (Maria), my brother (Frederick) and, not forgetting that sainted woman who rests on yonder hill (Rachel, who had died in 1915 and was buried in nearby Forest Hill Cemetery), it seems my lot to thank you all for this extraordinary demonstration. It is no easy matter to make you understand how much we appreciate it and how deeply touched we are by all you have done this day.' Mayor James D. Smith and other city officials said the new civic holiday would be an annual event. *Courtesy Oneida County Historical Society*

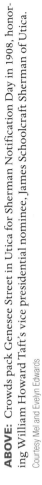

ABOVE: Crowds pack Genesee Street in Utica for Sherman Notification Day in 1908, honoring William Howard Taft's vice presidential nominee, James Schoolcraft Sherman of Utica.
Courtesy Mel and Evelyn Edwards

ABOVE: A Taft-Sherman banner flies above Genesee Street in Utica, circa 1908.
Courtesy Mel and Evelyn Edwards

RIGHT: Sherman Notification Day in 1908, honoring William Howard Taft's vice presidential nominee, James Schoolcraft Sherman of Utica.
Courtesy Mel and Evelyn Edwards

ABOVE: Welcome Home Day for World War I veterans at Oriskany Falls, August 16, 1919. Courtesy Oneida County Historical Society

LEFT: Crowds line the street as camels and circus wagons form a parade in Utica, circa 1918. Courtesy Mel and Evelyn Edwards

RIGHT: The garden club has a truck all decked out for a parade in Deansboro, circa 1920.
Courtesy Oneida County Historical Society

OPPOSITE: A group of marchers walk the parade route during the Utica Centennial celebration in 1932.
Courtesy Oneida County Historical Society

ABOVE: Baron von Steuben celebration, Remsen, 1931.
Courtesy Oneida County Historical Society

RIGHT: Dedication of the Gerrit Smith Tablet on Broad Street in Utica, July 30, 1932. Courtesy Oneida County Historical Society

ABOVE: Speeches take place during the Utica Centennial celebration in 1932.
Courtesy Oneida County Historical Society

RIGHT TOP: Family and friends wait for the start of the Utica Centennial celebration parade in 1932.
Courtesy Oneida County Historical Society

RIGHT BOTTOM: Onlookers line the streets of Utica to view the parade for the Utica Centennial celebration in 1932. *Courtesy Oneida County Historical Society*

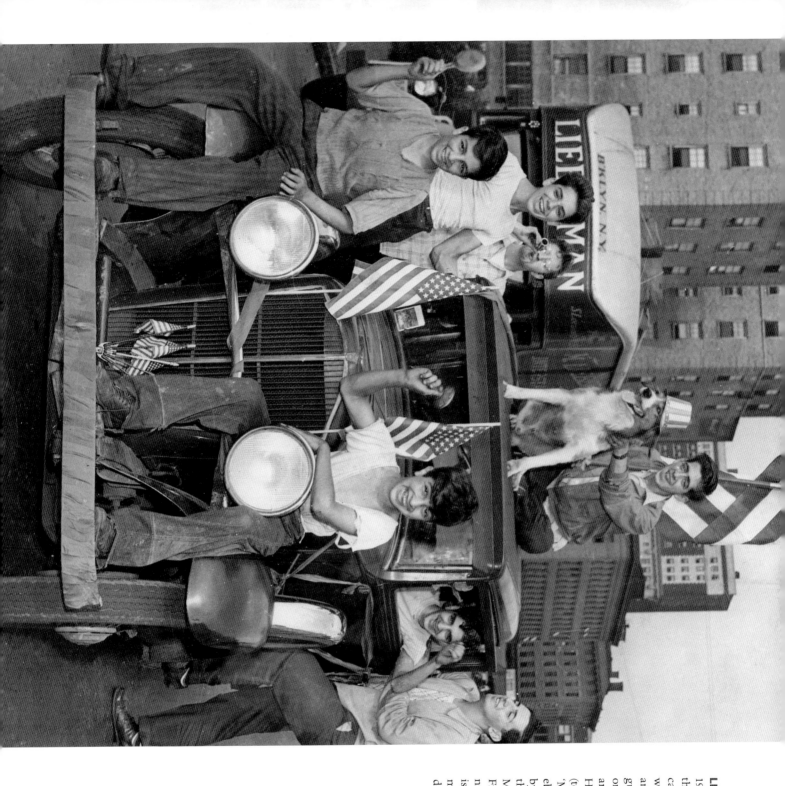

LEFT: Youngster climbed aboard a 1932 De-Vaux custom sedan to join thousands of other cars and trucks carrying happy Americans who were celebrating Japan's surrender and the end of World War II, August 14, 1945. Sitting on the fender on the left is Richard Mazloom, and behind him are Louis 'Joseph' Hage and Rudy Marchitelli. On the roof is 'Mark' Joseph with canine celebrant 'Chubby Marron,' owned by Fred 'Toots' Marron. Straddling the headlight on the right is Paul Mazloom, and behind him, driver Fred Mazloom and Tom Abounader. In the background, on left is Hotel Martin. It was reported more than 50,000 people jammed downtown Utica. *Courtesy Paul Mazloom*

LEFT: Joan Noonan rides as the queen of the Herkimer Sesquicentennial Parade in 1957. Noonan was crowned queen again for Herkimer's Bicentennial Parade in September 2007. *Courtesy Observer-Dispatch archives*

FAR LEFT: Parade in Utica shortly after Japan surrendered, 1945. *Courtesy Mrs. Isabella D. Bregnard*

BELOW: Captain Augustus J. Migell leads the Centennial Legion of Historic Military Commands down Genesee Street, Utica, 1958. *Courtesy Oneida County Historical Society*

Since our founding in 1898, **Adirondack Bank** has been dedicated to providing our customers with outstanding service, convenient locations, and competitive products. We strive to meet the requirements and financial goals of our customers as well as being a good neighbor in the communities we serve. And while we continue to grow, our dedication to customer satisfaction remains our number one priority, now and always.

Our success is achieved through the efforts of our talented and dedicated staff. We are a team of over 165 skilled professionals who live in your community and who actively participate in improving the quality of life for our families and our neighbors.

Adirondack Bank is here for you, as a personal and professional resource, to help you realize your dreams and achieve your goals.

ADIRONDACK BANK

Your Resource For Life.

| Utica | Whitesboro | Herkimer | Little Falls | Boonville | Old Forge | Lake Placid |
| Rome | Mohawk | Ilion | Holland Patent | Syracuse | Saranac Lake | Plattsburgh |

CLIENT SERVICES

315-ADKBANK or 1-877-404-BANK(2265)
adkbank.com

Member **FDIC**

EQUAL HOUSING LENDER

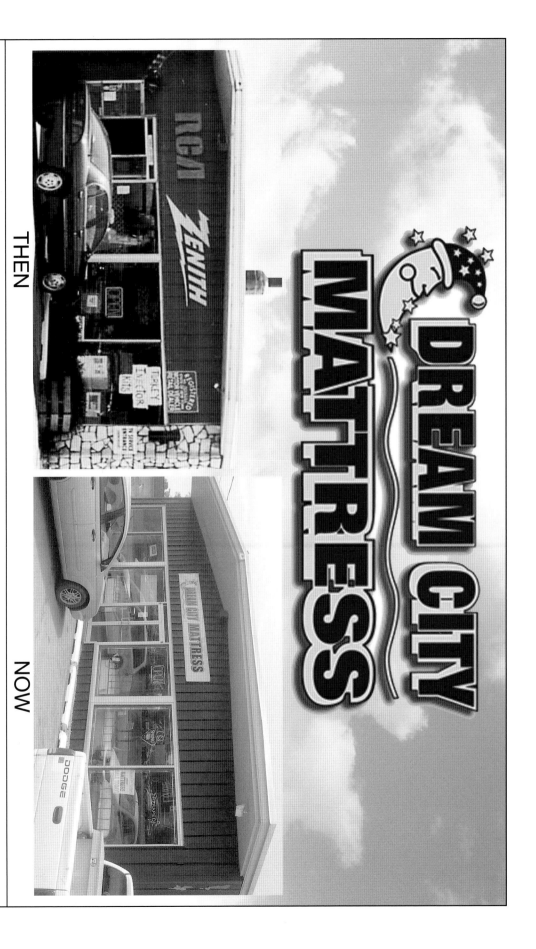

DREAM CITY MATTRESS

THEN

NOW

4670 Commercial Drive, New Hartford, NY 13413

(315)768-9000

Across from K-Mart

1239 Erie Blvd. West, Rome, NY 13440

(315)336-2500

Across from Lowe's

WWW.DREAMCITYMATTRESS.COM

Mike Jr's Auto Repair

1030 E. Dominick St., Rome, NY 13440

315-339-4830

Established in 1894 in Utica, NY, H.D. Morehouse & Son, now known as Morehouse Appliances, is one of the oldest surviving appliance retailers in New York state. First generation owner, Henry D. Morehouse started as a Blacksmith and Tinsmith. In addition to shoeing horses, he hammered tin and made stove pipe to earn a modest living. This progressed to selling used, and later new, coal and wood burning stoves. In the early 1900's, the business occupied their Columbia St. location, adding ice boxes to the mix at that time. The business took it's next major step in the early 20's

Circa Mid-1930's

when Leslie Morehouse, the son of Henry, added Maytag washers to their offerings. Morehouse Appliances is recognized as the second oldest Maytag dealer in the nation. Third generation owner, Henry, ushered in the advent of TV, selling some of the first televisions in the area. Currently operated by the fourth generation, the Morehouse family continues their tradition of providing superior customer service to central New Yorkers. These photos were taken of their Columbia Street storefront, they are now located in New Hartford.

1928 Sales Staff
Frank Carter | Chic Emerson | Marshall Longway
Leslie Morehouse | Jim Longway | Dick Richards

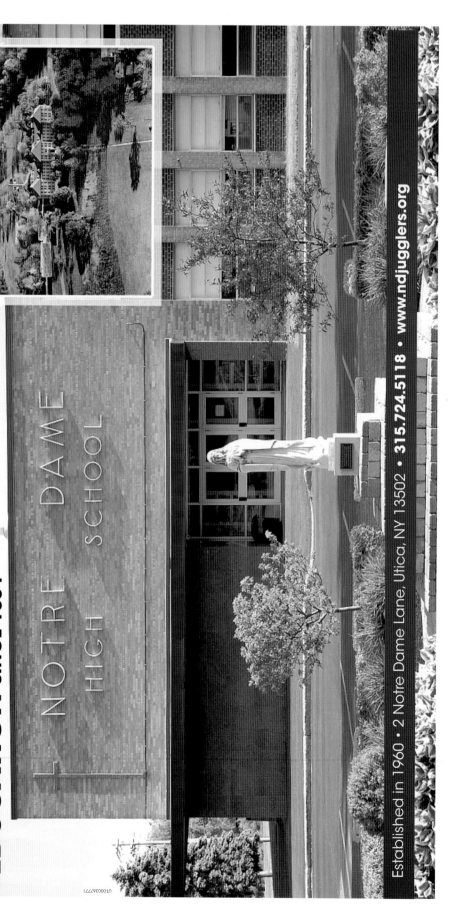

Notre Dame
Junior-Senior High School

CONTINUING THE TRADITION OF CATHOLIC EDUCATION SINCE 1834

UTICA CATHOLIC ACADEMY 1834-1976

ST. FRANCIS DE SALES 1907-1976

NOTRE DAME HIGH SCHOOL

Established in 1960 • 2 Notre Dame Lane, Utica, NY 13502 • 315.724.5118 • www.ndjugglers.org

124

"HERB" PHILIPSON'S

Outfitters for the Great Outdoors

It Started with Uncle Louie and Philipson's Army Navy Store in Utica... THE REST IS HISTORY!!

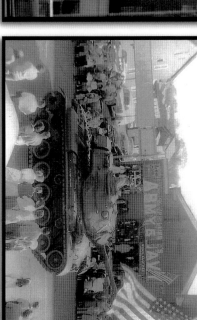

Gary Philipson, President

Uncle Louie worked in the Philipson's Army Navy Store that opened in the 1940's. This successful store became a downtown landmark for generations of Uticans.

In 1951, after serving in the Navy, "Herb" Philipson followed in his father's footsteps and opened the first "Herb" Philipson's Army Navy Store in Rome, NY.

That first store, a wooden structure, had a little over 800 square feet of selling space in a modest storefront location. It was replaced with a new building on the same site in 1957 before moving to its location on West Dominick in Rome. In 2009, it moved to a new beautiful, spacious modern location in The Plaza at Black River.

In 1970, "Herb" Philipson's expanded and opened its second store, in downtown Oneida, which moved in 2007 to a bigger store in the Glenwood Plaza in Oneida. A third store was added in the New Hartford Shopping Center in 1981, and a store in Herkimer opened in 1987. In 2003, a fifth store was opened in Watertown, and in 2007, "Herb" Philipson's was proud to open its sixth store in Liverpool, N.Y. In 2010 the 7th store was opened in Syracuse in the Western Lights Shopping Center.

Right from the start, Herb made a decision to offer famous name brands at low prices. With this philosophy, he gained a reputation as the "Price Fighter," even appearing in television commercials to parry imaginary prices in the boxing ring. After Herb passed away in 2003, his son Gary continued the proud family tradition of the "Herb" Philipson's Stores.

Rome • Oneida • Herkimer • New Hartford • Watertown • Liverpool • Syracuse

Hartman Flowers first opened it's doors on Palm Sunday in 1954 as a full service flower shop and in 1972 expanded to include a small antique shop in the back garage. In 1973, Don and Nancy Hartman took over the shop as Hartman Flowers and as the current owners the shop has evolved from the flower shop to the current full service Antique Shop with 3 full showrooms and 1,250 sq. ft. of showroom space, chocked full of quality antiques. When it comes to the antique business, owners Don and Nancy Hartman have over 40 years of experience in antiques as well as 35 years in the Estate & House sale business. They're also buyers of Gold & Silver coins, jewelry, & sterling flatware.

UT000348257

Committed to Excellence

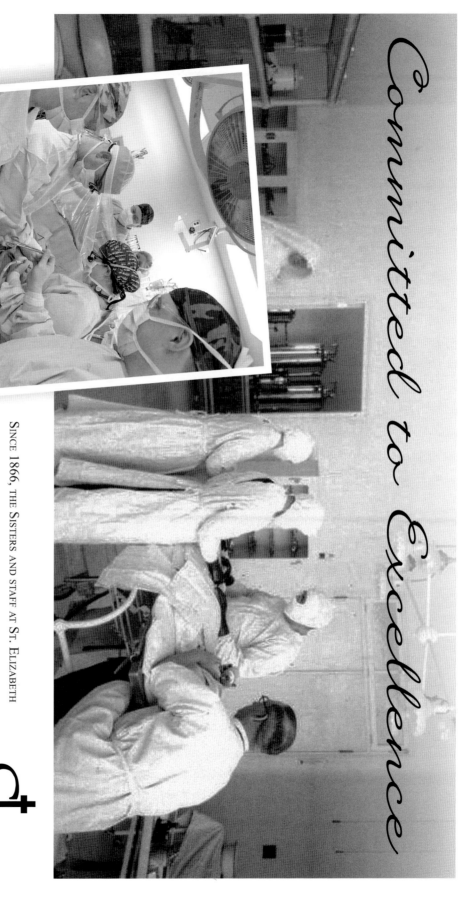

Since 1866, the Sisters and staff at St. Elizabeth Medical Center have been committed to excellence in healthcare and education, combining traditional values inspired by St. Francis of Assisi with the latest in medical technology.

S⁺F MC

www.stemc.org

TURNBULL INSURANCE SERVICE

ESTABLISHED IN UTICA, 1866.

James B. Turnbull walked from the Watertown area as an agent for Agricultural Insurance Company. He sold policies to farms and homes along the way and was appointed as an agent for the company in Utica. We continued to represent Agricultural for over 100 years, until they were sold to another company.

The photos show the office with James B. Turnbull, on the "Busy Corner" of Bleecker and Genesee Street in 1916. The other shows a street view of our offices at 240 Genesee St, Utica; with our large yellow and black sign on the building. One of the last signs to come down that hung over the sidewalks. We were on Genesee St for over 50 years.

The agency is now in the Fourth generation with James B. Turnbull IV and Mark A. Turnbull

In September 1949, Mr. John Trzepacz, my grandfather, opened Yorkville Memorials. With the help of the local "Polish" newspaper promoting a new entrepreneur he was able to sell his inventory – which in turn allowed him to purchase more inventory. With his success he was outgrowing his current location.

Wanting to keep the business growing he purchased land on Champlin Avenue in Yorkville, NY and constructed a building with a sandblast booth, an overhead crane, a new office, and an expanded display lot.

Being a family business he enlisted the help of his son's to work. They grew along with the business. In 1981 with the passing of my grandfather, the business began operation as a second generation business. In 2009, I am proud to say that I became the third generation of the Trzepacz family to own and operate Yorkville Memorials.

For over 60 years my family has manufactured and delivered numerous memorials. We pride ourselves on the quality of the craftsmanship, the superior grade of granite, and the excellent customer service we provide. A monument purchased from us will be delivered to the cemetery in a timely fashion.

We are a full service monument company that not only sells quality memorials, we offer our services at the time of passing to complete the final date. We also offer cleaning and repairs to keep your monument looking as good as the day it was placed in the cemetery.

We promise to serve you with honest, compassionate service for generations to come.

Gina Trzepacz Timpano (3rd Generation)

YORKVILLE MEMORIALS FIRST TRUCK
STUDEBAKER 1950

99 CAMPELL AVE.
DIAL-6-1781
YORKVILLE MEMORIALS

Since 1893...
We have been caring for people

2150 Bleecker Street, Utica

Proud to be
One of Oneida County's
Oldest Non-profit Corporations

This building was first built in 1875 and originally housed the No. 4 Fire station. This was the first and only fire house in the City of Utica's history to house three steamers which was the largest number by any engine company ever. These steamers included; a Cole Brother's Steamer in 1874, a Clap and Jones Steamer in 1884, and in 1906, the pride of the Department, an American "Metropolitan," three horse steamer.

In 1957, the City of Utica made a final decision to permanently close the No. 4 Fire station due to the cost of extensive repairs. The steamers, and Fireman were transferred to other Fire Stations in the Utica area.

In 1985 Michael G. Scarafile, President of Boscar Electric Co. Inc, bought the building and completely renovated the interior and exterior, along with adding more than 10,000 sq. ft. of additional warehouse space.

27 years later, Boscar Electric Co., Inc. still owns and operated it's Licensed Electrical Contractor and Consultant firm from this building.

UT-000366654

131

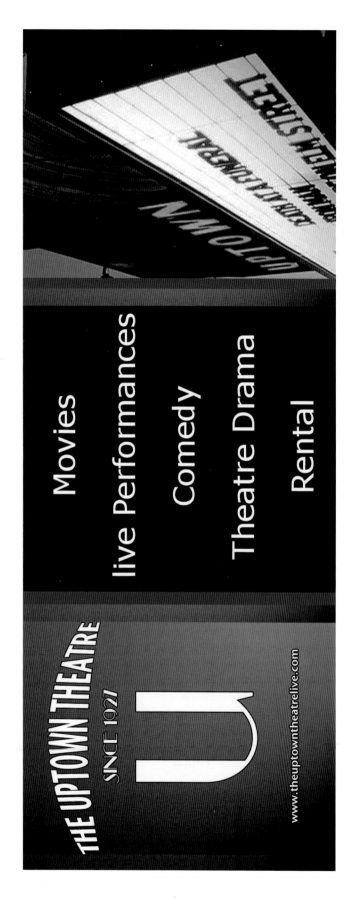

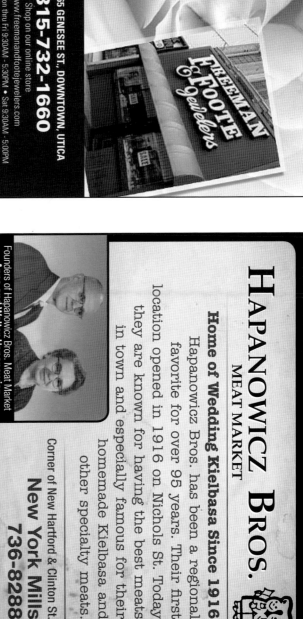

INDEX